I'll Be the Devil

Leo Butler was born in Sheffield in 1974. His first play, *Made of Stone*, was produced as part of the Royal Court Theatre Young Writers Festival in 2000. His other plays include *Redundant* (Royal Court Downstairs, 2001), winner of the George Devine Award for Most Promising Playwright; *Lucky Dog* (Royal Court Upstairs, 2004) and *The Early Bird* (Queens Theatre, Belfast, 2006), produced by Ransom Productions as part of the Belfast Festival. Other work includes two war plays for teenagers, *Devotion* (Theatre Centre, London, 2002) and *Heroes* (National Theatre, 2007). Leo Butler lives in London with his wife and daughter.

T0258337

Leo Butler

I'll Be the Devil

Methuen Drama

Published by Methuen Drama 2008

1 3 5 7 9 10 8 6 4 2

Methuen Drama
A & C Black Publishers Limited
38 Soho Square
London W1D 3HB
www.acblack.com

ISBN 978 1 408 10149 0

A CIP catalogue record for this book
is available from the British Library

Typeset by Country Setting, Kingsdown, Kent

For Beatrice

Acknowledgements

I'd like to thank Dominic Cooke for the original commission; the company of actors who took part in the reading of November 2006; my director, Ramin Gray, for being such an excellent partner-in-crime.

Huge thanks to Jeanie O'Hare for her meticulous guidance and for always believing in the play. And to Nazzi, without whom none of it would have been possible.

I'll Be the Devil was produced by the Royal Shakespeare Company and premiered at the Tricycle Theatre, London, on 21 February 2008. The cast was as follows:

Dermot	Tom Burke
Ellen	Samantha Young
Lieutenant Coyle	Eoin McCarthy
Maryanne	Derbhle Crotty
Lieutenant Ryan	Andrew Macklin
Sergeant Browne	Gerard Murphy
Captain Farrell	Edward MacLiam
Captain Skelton	JD Kelleher
Corporal O'Connor	Billy Carter
Lance Corporal Finnigan	Colm Gormley
Pot-Boy	David Toole
Colonel Fleming	John McEnery

Director Ramin Gray
Designer Lizzie Clachan
Lighting Designer Charles Balfour
Sound Designer Fergus O'Hare
Music Peter Cowdrey
Movement Anna Morrissey
Fights Philip d'Orleans
Assistant Director Jonathan Humphreys

I'll Be the Devil

Characters

Maryanne
Dermot, *Maryanne's son*
Ellen, *Maryanne's daughter*
Lieutenant Coyle, *Maryanne's lover*
Lieutenant Ryan, *Coyle's second*
Sergeant Browne
Captain Farrell
Captain Skelton
Corporal O'Connor
Lance Corporal Finnigan
Colonel Fleming, *an Englishman*
Pot-Boy
Fiddler
Piper

Setting

In and around Limerick, south-west Ireland. Two stormy
nights approaching Easter, 1762.

The scenes should flow effortlessly into each other, punctuated
by the storm. The play should be performed without an interval.

One

Dusk.

The hills.

Dermot *is placed in the stocks.*

It is a pillory, or 'standing stocks', resembling a crucifix. There is a small stool by the stocks.

Dermot*'s eyes have been gouged out. His clothes are rags, and he is covered with dried blood, cuts and bruises.*

Ellen *is crouched by him. She has a bucket and a cloth. She is washing his feet and legs.*

Dermot I saw the Devil last night, Ellen. He rode up out the Shannon on his horse. A great black Barbary she was, and him all burning red under his cloak. He asks me to sign his covenant with his claws pulled tight upon me throat. A dozen yellow eyes he has, a tongue the length of your arm. 'Not so long as I have breath in me head,' I says, 'Not so long as I can still draw blood. Get back under the earth,' I cry, 'and you take your stinking nag along with you!' Well, he didn't like that now, did he?

Ellen No.

Dermot He didn't like that.

Ellen He didn't like that, no.

Dermot Him all fallen from Heaven and I no better than ink without the pot, let alone the hand that drives it. Oh, the noise he made, Ellen. I swear he would've shook the Lord from off his cross had he sense enough to mark it, had I not been Saint of this rock. Had I not such a wealth of angels in me breast and not seen off his poison already.

Long pause.

Ellen.

Pause.

Ellen.

Ellen   Yes, Dermot?

Dermot   He spat in me ear, look.

Ellen   In your ear he spat?

Dermot   It was me brain he was aiming for.

Ellen   Oh.

Dermot   Can you not see?

Pause.

Ellen . . .

Ellen   It would take more than the Devil to clear a path through this filth.

Dermot   But I saw him, I tell you!

Ellen   And what would the Devil want with you?

Dermot   He thinks he has me fooled. He thinks he can drag me down through Purgatory.

Ellen   Oh, Dermot . . .

Dermot   The dirty beast.

Ellen   You're so stupid.

Dermot   You don't fool me, you old bastard, you can curse all you want! You can claw the flesh from off my bones for all the good it'll do you! You can choke on your own forked tongue, so help me God!

Long pause.

That'll teach him, won't it?

Pause.

That'll teach him though, won't it?

Pause.

Ellen . . .

A rumble of thunder. Long pause.

Ellen . . .

Ellen Would you stop . . . ?

Dermot Shhhh!

Ellen Stop wiggling your feet.

Dermot Do you not hear him?

Ellen I hear nothing.

Dermot Listen!

Ellen Oh, Dermot, come on . . .

Dermot He's calling us even now, my sister!

Ellen I'll never clean off this blood if you don't keep still.

Dermot But I swear to you, that's his mark.

Ellen Keep still I say!

Dermot Once he's shown himself the once, once he's found his way inside.

Ellen Just calm down and let me . . .

Dermot Tell me you'll pray for me, Ellen, please!

A burst of thunder. Long pause.

Ellen Have you emptied your bladder yet?

Pause.

Do you need the bucket, Dermot?

Pause.

There's no need to sulk now.

Dermot I'm not sulking.

Ellen You want to look the best for Our Lord.

Dermot (*mimics* **Ellen**)   'You want to look the best for Our Lord.'

Ellen   You're lucky they never cut your tongue out. The state of you, look. Blind as a beetle.

Dermot   And whose fault is that?

Ellen   You want to make a good impression. Don't you want that?

Pause.

You'll only upset Mammy.

Pause.

Dermot . . .

Dermot   He asked after you.

Pause.

Ellen   Dermot, please . . .

Dermot   He asked after you, he did.

Ellen   Oh now –

Dermot   He did!

Ellen   Don't be so –

Dermot   He called you by name, he did. 'Fetch me the midget,' he says. 'Fetch me the girl.'

Ellen   Dermot . . .

Dermot   'Fetch me the dwarf won't listen when she's spoken to and I'll roast her on me spit.'

Ellen   Dermot, please . . .

Dermot   'I'll roast her like a pig, just you see that I don't!'

Ellen   That's enough.

Dermot   'A dirty little piggy-wig sucking on her own filth!'

Ellen   If you won't keep –

Dermot   Get your hands off me!

Ellen   That's enough now, Dermot –

Dermot   Stop haunting me, pig!

Ellen   But I'm only –

Dermot   Oink oink oink!

Ellen   I only want to –

Dermot   Oink oink oink oink oink!

Ellen *throws the bucket of dirty water at* **Dermot***'s face.*

Long pause.

Dermot   Ellen . . .

Ellen   No.

Dermot   But you promised me, Ellen.

Ellen   I can't hear you.

Dermot   We have to believe –

Ellen   I can't hear you, Dermot, no!

Ellen *moves and sits on the grass, a distance apart from* **Dermot***.*

Long pause.

Dermot   There is such a thing though, isn't there?

Pause.

You do believe me though, don't you, girl?

Long pause.

Ellen.

Thunder and lightning.

Ellen, please.

It starts to rain.

I don't know what to believe.

Blackout.

Two

A mud cabin, built within the woods.

Night.

The storm, outside – thunder, lightning, heavy rain. Though the cabin has a roof, it cannot stop the rain from pouring in.

Maryanne *is sitting on the stool by the peat fire, plucking a chicken.*

Lieut Coyle *is standing by the open doorway. He is joined by* **Lieut Ryan**. *He carries an old hessian sack, in which is something big and heavy.*

Lieut Coyle   Where is he?

Maryanne   You're late.

Lieut Coyle   Don't play games with me now.

Maryanne   Oh, God forbid –

Lieut Coyle   I've warned you about that boy of yours.

Maryanne   – that I should quarrel with the palatine.

Lieut Coyle   Where is he?

Maryanne   You're letting the rain in.

Lieut Coyle   If you think I'm going to stand here . . .

Maryanne   Stand here like a mule can't hold his own piss.

Lieut Coyle   I'm warning you, Maryanne . . .

Maryanne   Shut the fucking door why don't you?!

Lieut Coyle *slams the door shut.*

Pause.

Lieut Coyle   Is that all right for you, lady of the house?

Maryanne   Fine.

Lieut Coyle   Do you mind if I take a look around?

Maryanne   Be my guest.

Lieut Coyle *doesn't move.*

Pause.

Maryanne   Is something the matter, Lieutenant?

Lieut Coyle   You know, you could save yourself a lot of time . . .

Maryanne   What?

Lieut Coyle   You could save yourself a lot of trouble . . .

Maryanne   You'll have to speak up, sir − what?

Lieut Coyle   If you would just tell me . . .

Maryanne   Dumb bastard, you.

Lieut Coyle   Are you trying to ruin me, woman?!

He throws the hessian sack on **Maryanne**'*s lap.*

Lieut Coyle   I should rip his rotten eyes out!

Maryanne (*peers into the sack*)   Is this for me, sir?

Lieut Coyle   In God's name . . .

Maryanne   Now you know I can't accept donations.

Lieut Coyle   Maryanne . . .

Maryanne   I suggest you seek indulgence elsewhere.

Lieut Coyle   Maryanne, please . . .

Maryanne   Preferably your arse.

Pause.

Lieut Coyle   Did you put him up to this?

Maryanne   She is a beauty, sir.

Lieut Coyle   What?

Maryanne   Oh yes, I can certainly see the resemblance.

She pulls a pig's severed head out of the sack.

One of your Londonderry cousins, I'm thinking.

Lieut Coyle All right now, just –

Maryanne One of your clan.

Lieut Coyle Maryanne . . .

Maryanne Is she Catholic or Protestant, I wonder?

Lieut Coyle I didn't come here to be mocked.

Maryanne What do you say, pig?

Lieut Coyle I'm warning you now.

Maryanne Are you a papal pig?

Lieut Coyle Look . . .

Maryanne Perhaps she'd care to take communion, sir.

Lieut Coyle If they find him . . .

Maryanne What's it to be?

Lieut Coyle If he so much as mentions my name!

Maryanne Would you like that, pig?

Lieut Coyle Do you know who this belonged to?!

He grabs the pig's head from **Maryanne**.

Lieut Coyle Do you know?!

Maryanne Now steady on, Lieutenant . . .

Lieut Coyle Jesus save us!

Maryanne There's no need to shout.

Lieut Coyle I told you he's not to go near that farm!

Maryanne And whose farm might that be, sir?

Lieut Coyle You know what I'm talking about.

Maryanne The farm you stole from me?

Lieut Coyle   It belongs to the military now.

Maryanne   The holy fucking surge.

Lieut Coyle   You know that, Maryanne, please!

Long pause.

Maryanne . . .

Maryanne   Yes, I see, sir, of course.

Lieut Coyle   Did you not tell him?!

Maryanne   I understand, sir.

Lieut Coyle   You've told him before what would happen.

Maryanne   The farm your Colonel obtained.

Lieut Coyle   You've warned him not to leave your side, you've done so.

Maryanne   The farm . . .

Lieut Coyle   The farm he's ransacked, woman!

Maryanne   The farm still reeks of my family's own blood.

Lieut Coyle   Take a look if you don't believe me! There are cattle scattered all over the land, Maryanne. Slaughtered, sodomised cattle – who else but that fucking lunatic?! Who else would do a thing like that – disfigured by the boy's own blade?! The stench itself would wake the dead, it's beyond human, Maryanne, he did this!

Pause.

Lieut Coyle   Maryanne . . .

Maryanne   You're foaming, Lieutenant.

Lieut Coyle (*wipes his mouth*)   You have to find him.

Maryanne   Do I?

Lieut Coyle   You have to find him and bring him home.

Maryanne   Is that an order?

Lieut Coyle   He's not to break the curfew.

Maryanne   You're threatening me.

Lieut Coyle   He's not to leave your side, that's the law.

Maryanne   Under whose authority?

Lieut Coyle   It's been the law for these past twenty years, woman, are you telling me it just slipped your mind?

Maryanne   Oh, then I must be punished, sir.

Lieut Coyle   What?

Maryanne   I see you've brought the fucking cavalry.

Pause.

Maryanne (*winks at* **Ryan**)   I clearly must be punished, sir, yes?

Lieut Coyle *hands the severed pig's head to* **Lieut Ryan**, *who exits, taking the pig's head with him.*

Maryanne   Of course I had hoped we might spend the evening together.

Lieut Coyle   For God's sake . . .

Maryanne   That we may keep each other warm, no?

Lieut Coyle   Is this any time . . . ?

Maryanne   Being only three days till Lent.

Lieut Coyle   What?

Maryanne   Penitence, sir. You will be joining in the fast, I trust?

Lieut Coyle   If you think I'm going to stand here and take orders . . .

Maryanne   It is the duty of every Catholic to forsake his belly over Easter.

Lieut Coyle   Maryanne . . .

Maryanne   You will be joining in the fast, sir.

Lieut Coyle   Where is he?

Maryanne   'Then was Jesus led into the wilderness to be tempted by the Devil. And when he had fasted forty days and forty nights, he was – '

Lieut Coyle   Maryanne, don't . . .

Maryanne   ' – afterward all hungered. And when the tempter came to – '

Lieut Coyle   For the love of God, don't do this to me!

Long pause.

Yes.

Maryanne   What?

Lieut Coyle   Yes, of course. Don't doubt my faith, Maryanne.

Maryanne   You were meant to be here three days ago.

Lieut Coyle   Look –

Maryanne   You laid your very life on it, sir.

Lieut Coyle   I haven't come here to –

Maryanne   Stuck in this hole without one scrap to call me own.

Lieut Coyle   And I am sorry, all right?

Maryanne   Without a single root to feed our children.

Lieut Coyle   I apologise, woman, can't you see – ?

Maryanne   You swore on the cross, Thomas!

Lieut Coyle   I have a regiment to keep, I can't just slip away –

Maryanne   Well, didn't you?!

Pause.

Lieut Coyle   Maryanne, please . . .

Maryanne   Under the bed.

Lieut Coyle   For Christ's sake, you're not even –

Maryanne   Under the bed, go on.

Lieut Coyle   I'm begging you –

Maryanne   Don't hurt my feelings now.

Lieut Coyle   Look at me, I'm –

Maryanne   The bed, go on!

Lieut Coyle *marches to the bed.*

Maryanne   Fat old Sassenach.

Lieut Coyle *frantically searches the blankets on the bed.*

Maryanne   Stick your head under.

Lieut Coyle   But –

Maryanne   Underneath, I said.

Lieut Coyle   There's nothing down there!

He overturns the bed. Long pause.

There's nothing down there.

Maryanne   Are you feeling better now, sir?

Lieut Coyle   Jesus Christ . . .

Maryanne   You should watch you don't injure yourself.

Lieut Coyle   Maryanne, don't . . .

Maryanne   A man of your standing.

Lieut Coyle   Don't make me . . .

Maryanne   A man of your weight.

Lieut Coyle   For the love of God!

Maryanne   You want to mind you don't damage your poor heart.

Lieut Coyle   Maryanne, please . . .

Maryanne   Fifty of your men come bursting through that door.

Lieut Coyle   Just let me talk to him.

Maryanne   I'd hate to be the one has to dig the fucking hole.

The storm blasts the cabin door open – crash!

Lieut Coyle *jumps, drawing his sword.*

He moves to the door and slams it shut, barring it with the bed.

Long pause.

Maryanne   Of course he won't be far away.

Lieut Coyle   What?

Maryanne   No, he won't stray too far, sir. He's no better than a dog when it comes to feeding, I'm sure you won't have to wait too long.

Pause.

Lieutenant . . .

Lieut Coyle   No.

Maryanne   You're not in any hurry, are you?

Pause.

Lieutenant, sir . . .

Lieut Coyle   I just told you, I'm not going anywhere, no! Dear God, woman, can you not answer a simple question?! I warned you before not to let him go out scavenging on his own, the matter was settled! I counted at least twenty dead pigs just now, he'll have us all in our graves if they catch him.

Maryanne   I should take that as a no then.

Lieut Coyle   He'll send us both to the hangman, don't you see? The Catholic is no better than a worm to those fiends, Maryanne. If he breathes one word, if they were to uncover my faith, if they discover my loyalty to you –

Maryanne   You call this loyalty!

Lieut Coyle   If they were to find the two of us here together like this. If they were to affiliate me with that madman.

Maryanne   Now that's no way to talk about the boy.

Lieut Coyle   The boy's an animal.

Maryanne   Your own son.

Lieut Coyle   He's no son of mine.

Maryanne   Well, I don't think –

Lieut Coyle   Not any more.

Maryanne   I don't think you have that choice, sir. Your children will bear your own coffin, I warrant, by spirit or by flesh.

Lieut Coyle   You know the rules, Maryanne.

Ellen (*hidden*)   Yes, sir.

Lieut Coyle   What?

Ellen (*hidden*)   Quite so, sir, yes.

Lieut Coyle   Are you . . . ?

Pause.

Are you trying to fucking . . . ?

Ellen (*hidden*)   Since you put it that way, sir –

Lieut Coyle *lifts up* **Maryanne**'s *skirt.* **Ellen** *is crouched between* **Maryanne**'s *legs, plucking a dead chicken.*

Ellen   I'm only too happy to oblige . . .

Lieut Coyle *drags* **Ellen** *out.*

Ellen   Ow!

Lieut Coyle   Would you look at the state of her?!

Ellen   Daddy, please!

Lieut Coyle   Jesus Christ . . .

Ellen   You're hurting me!

Lieut Coyle (*to* **Maryanne**)   Don't you have any decency?!

Ellen   Daddy . . .

Lieut Coyle (*to* **Maryanne**)   Well, don't you?!

Ellen   Daddy, please, my arm! Daddy . . .

Lieut Coyle (*to* **Maryanne**)   She's head to foot with it, look!

Maryanne *has returned to her stool, plucking the chicken.*

Lieut Coyle   I am addressing you, woman.

Maryanne   Oh come now, Lieutenant, it was only a bit of fun . . .

Lieut Coyle   Filth and mud and God knows what other excrement!

Ellen   Daddy, please, you're twisting my arm!

Lieut Coyle (*to* **Ellen**)   Look at me.

Ellen   It's hurting now, I can't . . .

Lieut Coyle (*to* **Ellen**)   Look at me, Ellen, give me your hand.

Ellen   But I thought you'd be pleased . . .

Lieut Coyle   Give me your hand now, come on.

He takes **Ellen** *by the hand and gets down on his knees.*

Lieut Coyle   Look to me, child.

Ellen   But I didn't mean –

Lieut Coyle   Look me in the eyes.

Ellen   But I didn't mean to make you so –

Lieut Coyle   Have you seen your brother? – Don't turn away now, come on.

Maryanne (*plucking her chicken*)   You're scaring the poor girl.

Lieut Coyle   Don't you lie to me now. You've seen him, haven't you?

Maryanne   Leave her alone, you big bully.

Lieut Coyle   Don't look to your mother – haven't I taught you not to tell tales?

Ellen   Yes, Daddy.

Lieut Coyle   Have I not taught you to follow the example of your patron saint?

Ellen   I know my place, Daddy, yes.

Lieut Coyle   Look at me.

Ellen   But I haven't –

Lieut Coyle   Look at me, Ellen, God help you!

He slaps **Ellen**.

Long pause.

Lieut Coyle   Ellen . . .

Ellen *starts to cry.*

Pause.

Lieut Coyle   Ellen, please, come on now, don't cry.

Pause.

Don't cry, Ellen . . .

Ellen (*crying*)   Get off me!

Lieut Coyle   Look –

Ellen (*crying*)   Get off me!

Lieut Coyle   You know I didn't mean to hurt –

Ellen (*crying*)   No!

Lieut Coyle   Oh, darling.

Ellen (*crying*)   I don't know what you're talking about.

Lieut Coyle   Come here.

Ellen (*crying*)   Daddy, no!

Lieut Coyle *locks* **Ellen** *in an embrace.*

Lieut Coyle   Come here, come on.

Lieut Coyle *kisses* **Ellen**'s *head.*

Lieut Coyle   That's it now. That's better.

Pause.

Daddy kiss it better.

Ellen   But I don't . . .

Lieut Coyle   Poor sweetheart.

Ellen (*crying*)   But I don't know what you mean . . .

Lieut Coyle   Poor mite, come here.

Ellen (*crying*)   I haven't seen anyone on the cross, I haven't.

Lieut Coyle   I know, darling, I know.

Ellen (*crying*)   I wanted to surprise you, Mammy said –

Lieut Coyle   I know, I'm sorry.

Ellen (*crying*)   Mammy said we were to give you a welcome home.

Lieut Coyle   Yes, and you've done so, Ellen . . .

Ellen (*crying*)   That I might help cheer you. That I might sit you down by the fire and help to dry you off from the storm.

Lieut Coyle   Oh, my darling, you know that I wouldn't –

Ellen (*crying*)   That we might pray together for Easter.

Lieut Coyle   And we will, Ellen, we will, come on now, please. You know I wouldn't dream of hurting you, don't you?

Ellen *cries.*

Lieut Coyle   You know that, don't you, girl?

He kisses **Ellen**.

Lieut Coyle   You know that deep down?

Ellen (*crying*)   Yes, Daddy.

Lieut Coyle   'For in thee, O Lord, do I put my trust: let me never be put to confusion. Deliver me in thy righteousness and cause me to escape: incline thine ear unto me, and save me.'

Pause.

You remember the verse I taught your brother and you both?

Ellen   Yes, of course.

Lieut Coyle   'For thou . . . '

Ellen   'For thou art my rock and salvation.'

Lieut Coyle   Then you remember the oaths we took.

Ellen   Yes, I know, but –

Lieut Coyle   Then you can forgive me, can't you?

Ellen   But I didn't –

Lieut Coyle   Say you'll forgive me, darling.

Maryanne (*plucking her chicken*)   Oh, she forgives you all right. She'll forgive the very Devil, won't you, girl?

Lieut Coyle   Say it, Ellen, for the love of God.

Maryanne   I would place her among the saints were I pontiff.

Lieut Coyle (*embraces* **Ellen**)   Ellen, please . . .

Maryanne   The virtue in her.

Lieut Coyle   Say that you forgive your father.

Maryanne   Though Christ knows where she gets it.

Lieut Coyle (*to* **Maryanne**)   Would you stop . . . ?

Maryanne   I often wonder if she fell from Heaven, sir.

Lieut Coyle   I'm talking to her!

Maryanne   Coming from your spineless cock −

Lieut Coyle   Maryanne!

Maryanne   − it must surely be some miracle.

Lieut Coyle   For God's sake, can't you keep your mouth shut for five minutes?!

The door bursts open; the bed that is propped up against it falls.

Lieut Ryan *enters, dragging a slaughtered pig tied to a rope.*

Lieut Ryan   Dead pig, sir.

Lieut Coyle   What?!

Lieut Ryan   Dead pig.

Lieut Coyle   I can see what it is!

Maryanne (*to* **Ellen**)   Come here, darling, come here.

Ellen *scrambles over to* **Maryanne**.

Over the following, **Maryanne** *spits on her sleeve and cleans* **Ellen**'s *face, head and hands with it.*

Lieut Coyle (*to* **Ryan**)   Jesus Christ, Ryan, you don't have to drag it around like an old bagpipe!

Lieut Ryan   But, sir, I didn't know what else to −

Lieut Coyle   Where was it?

Lieut Ryan   What?

Lieut Coyle   Where did you find it?

Lieut Ryan   Oh . . .

Lieut Coyle   Won't you speak?

Lieut Ryan   Oh, yes, sir.

Lieut Coyle   I suppose it just slipped out your arse, did it?

Lieut Ryan   No, I found it on the pass just now, sir, I think ...

Lieut Coyle   You think.

Lieut Ryan   Sir, please, it wasn't there before.

Lieut Coyle   Did you see anyone?

Lieut Ryan   It's still breathing, look.

Lieut Coyle   When I ask a question, Lieutenant ...

Lieut Ryan   If you would just let me answer ...

Lieut Coyle   Was there a trail?

Pause.

Lieut Ryan   Sir, please ...

Lieut Coyle   Were there footprints?

Lieut Ryan *hesitates.*

Lieut Coyle   Were there footprints, Lieutenant? Speak!

Lieut Ryan   I don't remember.

Lieut Coyle   What?

Lieut Ryan   I don't recall.

Lieut Coyle   Did you even look?

Lieut Ryan *hesitates.*

Lieut Coyle   For God's sake, man!

Lieut Ryan   Sir, please, you can't –

Lieut Coyle   You must have seen something!

Lieut Ryan   Lower your voice.

Lieut Coyle   What?

Lieut Ryan   Lower your voice, sir, you can't speak to me like that.

Lieut Coyle   Are you trying to – ?

Lieut Ryan   You can't speak to me like a common –

Lieut Coyle *hits* **Lieut Ryan** *across the head.*

Lieut Ryan   Aah!

Lieut Coyle *grabs* **Lieut Ryan** *and drags him aside.*

Lieut Coyle   I'll speak to you as I choose.

Lieut Ryan   No, please . . .

Lieut Coyle   Threaten me in front of these fucking
peasants, have you lost your senses, boy? Can't you see what
we're up against?

Lieut Ryan   I can see with my own two eyes –

Lieut Coyle   You see what I bid thee, Ryan, and nothing
more. Don't think for one moment that there's any truth in
what this woman claims. (*Laughs.*) That I would in any way be
bound to a Catholic!

Lieut Ryan   Well, are you, sir?

Lieut Coyle *strikes* **Lieut Ryan.**

Lieut Ryan   Aah!

Lieut Coyle   That is treason, Lieutenant!

Lieut Ryan   Sir, please, you can't –

Lieut Coyle   What, am I your ensign?

He strikes **Lieut Ryan.**

Lieut Ryan   Aah!

Lieut Coyle   Come at me with your poison! For how long
have we been sworn?

Lieut Ryan   But, sir –

Lieut Coyle   For how long, Lieutenant Ryan?

Lieut Ryan   Please, I'll tell my uncle!

Lieut Coyle   You'll what?

Lieut Ryan   I'll tell my uncle, sir, please, you can't speak to me like this!

Lieut Coyle   Are you my second or aren't you?

Lieut Ryan   My family own two-fifths of this land, I will not be treated like a common soldier.

Lieut Coyle   Your family saw fit to put you under my command, Ryan.

Lieut Ryan   But it is −

Lieut Coyle   That was their wish.

Lieut Ryan   It is improper, sir, please!

Lieut Coyle   Are you my second, boy? − Answer!

Lieut Ryan   Of course, sir, just −

Lieut Coyle   Then you will do as you are bid, you will learn by example.

Lieut Ryan   Example!

Lieut Coyle   The example of my stripes, you belligerent seed, you sapling. What? Do they frighten you?

Lieut Ryan   Frighten me?

Lieut Coyle   Do the spirits of the forest frighten you, Lieutenant? The ghosts and foul demons that wait among the trees? Why, they'll set a man against his wits if he dares not stand firm. Are you to be held to ransom by a pagan's superstition?

Lieut Ryan   No, I mean −

Lieut Coyle   Or will it be Luther you follow? Oh, come on, Lieutenant, you're shaking in your boots, look.

Lieut Ryan   I mean, yes, sir, of course, quite right!

Lieut Coyle   Well, don't just stand there, fool!

Lieut Ryan   Sir!

Lieut Coyle   Find out who did this! Go on with you!

Lieut Ryan *exits.*

Lieut Coyle   Jesus save us all . . .

Ellen   Is Daddy not well?

Maryanne   Oh no, child.

Lieut Coyle (*at the pig*)   Are you out of your fucking mind?!

Maryanne   No, it's just the excitement of Easter, he'll soon calm down.

Lieut Coyle (*takes his dagger*)   Pity the poor swine!

Maryanne   Isn't that so, Lieutenant?

Lieut Coyle   Jabbing at its brain like he was trying to free its very conscience. Did you not train him how to use a knife?

Maryanne   That's your duty.

Lieut Coyle   Could he not have shown a little mercy at least?!

Maryanne   Lieutenant . . .

Lieut Coyle   This is how you kill a pig!

Lieut Coyle *cuts the pig's throat. The pig squeals.*

Squatting over the dead pig, **Lieut Coyle** *catches his breath.*

The storm continues.

Long pause.

Ellen   Should I sing the song now, Mammy?

Long pause.

Mammy.

Maryanne   Oh, that would be lovely, darling.

Ellen (*to* **Coyle**)   Mammy taught me a hymn.

Lieut Coyle (*to* **Maryanne**)   You sent him, didn't you?

Ellen   Would you like to hear it?

Pause.

Ellen   Daddy . . .

Lieut Coyle (*to* **Maryanne**)   You sent him.

Ellen   Daddy, please . . .

Lieut Coyle   It was you, Maryanne, you did this!

Maryanne (*to* **Ellen**)   Go and get into place now.

Lieut Coyle   If you think –

Maryanne (*to* **Ellen**)   Go on, child.

Lieut Coyle   If you expect me to stand before the Colonel and defend him –

Maryanne (*to* **Ellen**)   By the fire, remember?

Lieut Coyle   Maryanne!

Maryanne   Let her sing you her song, you old bastard, she's been waiting for you all day.

Pause.

Ellen *moves and stands by the peat fire.*

Lieut Coyle   Maryanne, please, you must –

Maryanne (*to* **Ellen**)   Take a deep breath now, go on.

Lieut Coyle   You must know that I can't –

Maryanne   Sit down, Lieutenant!

Lieut Coyle   I can't just relinquish my own company for the sake –

Maryanne   For the sake of your daughter! Well?!

Lieut Coyle *hesitates, then slams the cabin door shut and sits on the edge of the makeshift bed.*

Long pause.

Ellen (*sings*)
  Oh Paddy dear, and did you hear the news that's going
    round?
  The shamrock is by law unfit to grow on Irish ground,
  No more St Patrick's Day we'll keep, his colour can't be seen,
  For there's a cruel law against . . .

Maryanne/Ellen (*sing*)
  . . . the wearing of the green!

Maryanne *applauds* **Ellen.**

Maryanne   Oh, well, isn't she the angel!

Maryanne *motions for* **Lieut Coyle** *to applaud.*

Maryanne   Hasn't she the prettiest little voice! Hasn't she
though? Oh!

Lieut Coyle *applauds.* **Maryanne** *lifts up* **Ellen** *and kisses her.*

Maryanne   That was wonderful, darling!

Ellen   Thank you, Mammy.

Maryanne   Take a bow now, come on.

Ellen *bows.*

Maryanne (*applauds*)   Oh, look at her!

Ellen   Was that all right, Daddy?

Lieut Coyle   Yes . . .

Ellen   Could you hear every word?

Maryanne   We could hear the parchment it was set upon,
my love.

Ellen   Daddy . . .

Lieut Coyle   Yes, it was lovely, darling.

Maryanne (*to* **Ellen**)   You see, what did I tell you?

Lieut Coyle   Thank you.

Maryanne (*to* **Ellen**)   I told you he'd be pleased, didn't I?

Ellen   Would you like me to teach it?

Lieut Coyle   Oh . . . Oh, well . . .

Ellen   We could sing it together.

Lieut Coyle   Well, I don't think . . .

Ellen   That's right though, isn't it, Mammy?

Lieut Coyle   Maybe some other time.

Maryanne   Oh, don't be such a stuffed bull, Lieutenant . . .

Ellen   Daddy, please . . .

Lieut Coyle (*to* **Maryanne**)   I think you'd better . . .

Maryanne   . . . let her teach you her song, come on.

Ellen (*to* **Coyle**)   We could sing a line each then, couldn't we?

Lieut Coyle   Maybe some other time, Ellen.

Ellen   We could sing it on the boat.

Maryanne   Now that's a clever idea!

Ellen   We could sing it as we leave port.

Maryanne   That's right.

Ellen   We could . . .

Maryanne   We could sing it on the boat, couldn't we, Lieutenant?

Long pause.

Lieut Coyle   What?

Maryanne   Couldn't we just!

Lieut Coyle   What boat?

Maryanne   Have you not heard?

Ellen   The boat sailing for England.

Maryanne   That's right, Ellen, we saw it from the top field, didn't we? Why, you can almost hear it – listen. The wind on the sails. The rattle of the cannon upon the salted Shannon air.

Ellen   Mammy says there'll be angels waiting for us.

Maryanne   On the deck, Ellen, that's right. On the deck and in the crow's nest, a whole regiment of angels. Surely you've heard, Lieutenant?

Ellen   The Angel Gabriel.

Maryanne   You saw him in a dream, didn't you, girl?

Ellen   He steered the ship himself.

Lieut Coyle   Did he now?

Maryanne   Tell him about the mountains. You remember the snowy mountains, don't you, Ellen?

Ellen   Oh . . .

Maryanne   Reaching up through the clouds.

Lieut Coyle   Let her finish.

Ellen   Yes, Mammy, I do.

Maryanne   They do be lining the coast from Argyll to Land's End.

Ellen (*to* **Coyle**)   And we can see them in the distance.

Maryanne   They're in the distance and as we drop anchor . . .

Pause.

Maryanne   And as we drop anchor – come on now, girl, you remember.

Ellen   I don't . . .

Maryanne   You remember the Virgin Mary.

Ellen   Oh . . . Oh, yes.

Maryanne (*to* **Coyle**)   She'll forget her own mind.

Ellen   That's right, Mammy.

Maryanne   Waiting in her carriage to lead us safely home.

Ellen   To Buckingham Palace.

Maryanne (*to* **Coyle**)   It's so easy to forget in all this excitement.

Lieut Coyle   Quite.

Ellen   Mammy says I'll have my own maid.

Maryanne   You can have anything you want, my girl.

Ellen   Will I not have to bathe in the river any more?

Maryanne   We will be bathed in milk.

Ellen   Will we not have to work until nightfall?

Maryanne (*laughs*)   Work! What work?! The work of a fat old Persian cat, I grant you!

Ellen   Might we have our own roof? A roof with real wooden walls?

Maryanne   Well, if we pray very hard . . .

Ellen   Might I have a bed of my own?

Maryanne   You might want to ask your . . .

Ellen   Daddy.

Pause.

Ellen   Daddy . . .

Lieut Coyle   No.

Ellen   Will brother Dermot be with us?

Long pause.

Daddy . . .

Lieut Coyle (*to* **Maryanne**)   That's no hymn for a child.

Ellen   Have I said something wrong?

Pause.

Lieut Coyle   Of course not, darling.

Ellen   Did I speak the wrong line?

Maryanne   Now come on, Ellen, don't be tiring out your father.

Ellen   But I only –

Maryanne   Travelling all that way from town – (*To* **Coyle**.) I'm surprised you're not flat on your back, Lieutenant.

Lieut Coyle   Now don't you –

Maryanne (*to* **Ellen**)   I'm surprised he's not face down in a puddle!

Lieut Coyle   Don't push me, Maryanne.

Maryanne   How you'll fare against the French is a mystery to me.

Lieut Coyle   What?

Maryanne   The French, sir.

Lieut Coyle   Now, listen –

Maryanne   How you'll manage in battle – by my foot, I can only pray you've got the blessing of King George. Though I do hear you'll be flanked by the Prussian Army at least.

Lieut Coyle   Who told you?

Maryanne   And whose banner will you bear, I wonder?

Lieut Coyle   Maryanne . . .

Maryanne   The red, white and blue?

Lieut Coyle   I'm not –

Maryanne   The green perhaps?

Lieut Coyle   I'm not playing your –

Maryanne   The orange!

Will it be the orange, Lieutenant?

Pause.

Lieutenant . . .

Lieut Coyle   Who told you?

Who was it?

Maryanne   We will pray for you, of course. In the Abbey.

Lieut Coyle   What?

Maryanne   Westminster Abbey. (*To* **Ellen**.) We'll ask the Pope for salvation, won't we, child?

Ellen   Yes, Mammy.

Maryanne   We'll call on Jesus to bring the enemy to his knees.

Ellen   Oh, yes, that's right . . .

Maryanne   To see him safely home.

Ellen   To the Palace.

Maryanne   To the light and love of Old England.

Well?

What do you think, Lieutenant? Is it a good plan?

Long pause.

Thomas . . .

Lieut Coyle   You want to watch what you say.

Maryanne   Now don't disappoint the poor girl.

Lieut Coyle   You should be mindful what you teach.

Maryanne   Go on, Ellen, the token.

Ellen   I kept a token for you, look.

She removes a chain that is fastened round her neck. On it hangs a crucifix.

Look, Daddy.

She offers the chain/crucifix to **Lieut Coyle**.

Ellen   To protect you, look.

Pause.

You can wear it round your neck.

Lieut Coyle   Yes, that's . . .

Ellen   To remind you that I'll always be with you. Won't you take it?

Pause.

Daddy . . .

Lieut Coyle   Run along now.

Ellen   Don't you like it?

Lieut Coyle   Run along, go on.

Ellen   But . . .

Lieut Coyle   Go and say your prayers, there's a good girl.

Ellen   But I saved it . . .

Lieut Coyle   It's way past your bedtime, Ellen, that's enough.

Ellen   But I saved it for you.

Lieut Coyle   Go on now.

Ellen   Daddy, look, I –

Lieut Coyle   Go on!

Lieut Coyle *snatches the chain/crucifix from* **Ellen**.

Ellen   Daddy, please!

Maryanne   Answer the girl.

Lieut Coyle (*to* **Maryanne**)   You know they'll drown you in the river just for having this alone!

Maryanne   Oh, come now, Lieutenant, she only meant –

Lieut Coyle   She meant nothing, Maryanne!

Ellen You can keep my missal.

Lieut Coyle What?

Ellen My missal.

She takes a missal from her pocket, offering it to **Lieut Coyle**.

Ellen My prayer book, Daddy, you can read it on the battlefield.

Lieut Coyle Jesus Christ . . .

Ellen You can call on the saints to protect you –

Lieut Coyle (*snatches the missal*) That's an order, child!

Ellen To protect you from all evil –

Lieut Coyle Wait outside, for the love of God! For the love of God –

He whisks **Ellen** *out of the cabin door, shutting it up behind her.*

Lieut Coyle – that you should have ever been born, wait outside, I say!

Maryanne Will your wife be joining you?

Lieut Coyle What?

Maryanne You heard me.

Long pause.

She moves to the peat fire, and removes the pot from the fire. She ladles the potato stew from out of the pot and into a small bowl.

Will your wife be joining you, Lieutenant?

Lieut Coyle Look . . .

Maryanne The anticipation must be almost too much to bear. A woman of her years.

Lieut Coyle All right . . .

Maryanne A woman of her size. Have they cleared an extra deck for her, Lieutenant?

Lieut Coyle   You leave her out of this.

Maryanne   She has her own galleon, no? I imagine her family could afford a whole fleet if they so pleased.

Maryanne   Coming from such Cromwellian stock.

Lieut Coyle   That's enough.

Maryanne   Is she a saint, I wonder?

Lieut Coyle   Maryanne . . .

Maryanne   To marry a poor peasant like you.

Lieut Coyle   Don't . . .

Maryanne   That's some act of charity!

Long pause.

That is charity indeed.

Pause.

She must think she has you trained like one of her miserable pooches.

Lieut Coyle   All right . . .

Maryanne   She'll have you auctioned the moment you reach shore.

Lieut Coyle   Maryanne . . .

Maryanne   A symbol of the Commonwealth no less. A trophy of their good works.

Lieut Coyle   She's a good woman.

Maryanne   Is she joining you?

Lieut Coyle   She's more virtue than you'll ever know.

Maryanne   Your horse?

Lieut Coyle   What?

Maryanne   Are you taking your horse?

Pause.

Are you taking your horse, sir?

Lieut Coyle   Maryanne . . .

Maryanne   Crawl away.

Lieut Coyle   What?

Maryanne   Break the girl's heart.

Long pause.

Lieut Coyle   She's a sweetheart.

Maryanne   She's right.

Lieut Coyle   She needs protecting, she doesn't –

Maryanne   She's a vision of fucking purity, any fool can see that.

Lieut Coyle   She doesn't deserve to have her mind played tricks with.

Maryanne   Did you think you could just creep away?

Lieut Coyle   It's up to you to protect her, Maryanne.

Maryanne   Do you not care about your daughter?

Lieut Coyle   Of course I care!

Maryanne   Does it not matter if she rots?

Lieut Coyle   I don't have any choice, woman!

Maryanne   Oh, I see.

Lieut Coyle   A man must have reason, he must have order.

Maryanne   Oh, well . . .

Lieut Coyle   Regardless of faith! There must be political order, Maryanne.

Maryanne   Well, since you put it that way, sir.

Lieut Coyle   Believe me . . .

Maryanne I am enlightened.

Lieut Coyle Believe me, if I could place you in the squadron I would. If I could plant a beard on your chin and teach you how to use a sword. If by holy conversion alone you might be saved from this poverty, and if –

Maryanne If I were an oaf like you.

Lieut Coyle Is this the suit of an oaf? Is this colour and purse . . . ?

Maryanne You're nothing but a farmer, Coyle.

Lieut Coyle What?

Maryanne You're a trained monkey, that's all.

Lieut Coyle For Christ's sake . . .

Maryanne Stand aside while your own family starves.

Lieut Coyle You can't seriously expect me to hide in a quarry like the rest of you fucking animals.

Maryanne Oh, animals now, is it?

Lieut Coyle Well, can you?!

Maryanne Oh no, sir.

Lieut Coyle Maryanne . . .

Maryanne An animal would never betray his own kind.

Lieut Coyle Have I not kept you in food and water for the past God knows how many years? Have I not lent you money and clothes? When my brother died, I swore that I'd take care of you.

Maryanne Oh, you took care of me all right.

Lieut Coyle That's right, woman, I kept my promise, no matter whose side we're on. Do you think you would even be here if I hadn't took the oath? I gave you children, for God's sake, what more proof do you need?! When they moved you off the farm, did I not leave you with the little they would have

otherwise burnt? They would have thrown you all on the fire
had I not pleaded with them. Had I not begged and threatened
my own standing, and for what?! For you to set that madman
loose and to blackmail me with your own daughter?

Maryanne   She's your daughter too.

Lieut Coyle   Is this what you teach her?

Maryanne   Teach her, Lieutenant?

Lieut Coyle   You're out to punish me!

Maryanne   Oh no, sir, I know my rights.

Lieut Coyle   Maryanne . . .

Maryanne   I've spent a lifetime under Penal Law, I know
my place.

Lieut Coyle   If you think for one moment –

Maryanne   The Catholic does not trespass upon occupied
land, Lieutenant. The Catholic does not trade, rent, lease and
he surely does not steal from the property of his betters, let
alone butcher the swine that keeps it.

Lieut Coyle   Oh, then forgive me my fucking . . .

Maryanne   There's no doubt to be found in me, sir.

Lieut Coyle   No doubt!

Maryanne   The Catholic does not exercise his religion,
neither will he receive education. He will not enter a profession,
nor will he hold public office. He will not buy or lease any
land, and God forbid that he should vote. – Would you like me
to go on? The Catholic will not bear Catholic children, and he
shall be fined should he not attend the Protestant church. He
shall not carry gun, pistol or sword under penalty of fine,
pillory or public whipping. He will be fined and executed
should he own a horse for over the alloted sum – that's five
pounds to you and me, Lieutenant, we all remember that. He
will not own a horse, nor will he receive a gift or inheritance
from any man, least of all the Protestant. He shall serve the

Protestant at his command, but he shall not live within five miles of one. He shall not live near town nor village nor shit upon the soil unless he wish to kiss the hangman. He shall not live at all, sir. No, I am indeed schooled in that solemn verse, I know where my allegiance lies.

Lieut Coyle   Your allegiance lies to no one, filth.

Maryanne   This same filth bore you children, Lieutenant. Do you think I would dare jeopardise the only thing I have left?

Lieut Coyle   I know what I see before me.

Maryanne   The Treaty of Limerick was passed some hundred years ago, Lieutenant. I've had a lifetime and beyond to know my rights. If your brother had not betrayed the law of English, had he not had your strength . . .

Lieut Coyle   Don't you breathe a word about that man.

Maryanne   He was my husband, Thomas!

Lieut Coyle   I've told you before –

Maryanne   Had he not been too weak to play your dirty game and keep up this pretence –

Lieut Coyle   That's enough!

Maryanne   We would be living on that farm to this day, Thomas – do you think I don't know that?

Lieut Coyle   All right –

Maryanne   The rebellion died at the sword of Oliver Cromwell, do you think I would sacrifice this poor girl's soul for that – for what? For the will and charity of the Roman Catholic Church?

Lieut Coyle   No, of course not.

Maryanne   Should I send her to the gallows for that hollow cause?

Lieut Coyle   Look . . .

Maryanne   Should I do that, Thomas?

Lieut Coyle   If they were to find her with this –

He pulls out the chain/crucifix.

– Catholic filth, it is forbidden! What, should I brand it on her fucking hide?!

Maryanne   You can't deny the girl her faith, sir.

Lieut Coyle   Do you want her to grow into her brother? Is that what you want?

Maryanne   The boy's madness is your doing.

Lieut Coyle   I can only pray he hasn't corrupted her already.

Maryanne   Well, if you were ever home to protect the poor thing.

Lieut Coyle   What?

Maryanne   If you were ever home . . .

Lieut Coyle   We're at war, for Christ's sake!

Maryanne   And whose war is that, sir?

Lieut Coyle   Oh, come on, Maryanne . . .

Maryanne   You overfed eunuch.

Lieut Coyle   If you would just stop . . .

Maryanne   You Negro.

Lieut Coyle   Stop . . .

Maryanne   You piss-grovelling growth on the cock-end of the Commonwealth.

Long pause.

Have I said something to offend you?

Pause.

Lieutenant.

Lieut Coyle   Hold out your hand.

Maryanne   What?

Lieut Coyle   Your hand.

He puts the crucifix back in his pocket, and, at the same time, removes his purse.

Pause.

Give me your hand.

Maryanne   Oh . . .

Lieut Coyle   For the girl.

Maryanne   That's very thoughtful of you, sir.

Lieut Coyle *empties his purse onto* **Maryanne***'s hand.*

Lieut Coyle   Three guineas.

Maryanne   Well, I . . .

Lieut Coyle   Keep it.

Maryanne   I'm lost for words, Lieutenant.

Lieut Coyle   Are you going to tell me where he is?

Maryanne   Three guineas.

Lieut Coyle   The boy.

Maryanne   For an old papist whore.

Lieut Coyle   Tell me.

Maryanne (*counting the coins*)   You might purge the living Devil with this.

Lieut Coyle   Where might I find him?

Pause.

Maryanne, come on now . . .

Maryanne   And will you grant her liberty?

Lieut Coyle   What?

Maryanne   Will you grant the girl her freedom, sir?

Lieut Coyle   Look . . .

Maryanne   Will you do that?

Lieut Coyle   Woman, please, I have never –

Maryanne   There must be some space on that boat of yours.

Lieut Coyle   I have never promised –

Maryanne   There must be somewhere we could hide.

Lieut Coyle   In all our time together –

Maryanne   In the name of Jesus, will you not find some way for your own flesh and blood?

Lieut Coyle   You can't expect me –

Maryanne   Will you not consider it, even?

Lieut Coyle   Maryanne –

Maryanne   Will you do that for me, even?

Lieut Coyle   Maryanne, please –

Maryanne   Will you do that, Thomas? – Answer me!

Long pause.

Lieut Coyle   Maryanne . . .

Maryanne   Then you would forget the love we shared . . .

Lieut Coyle   What?

Maryanne   Then you would deny all tenderness, no?

Long pause.

Lieut Coyle   Maryanne, please.

Pause.

He touches **Maryanne** *tenderly by her shoulders.*

Lieut Coyle   Please, you know if there was any other way . . .

Maryanne   Of course she would make a beautiful young bride.

Lieut Coyle   What?

Maryanne   She would make a fine bride, sir.

Pause.

Lieut Coyle   What?

Maryanne   One of your honest English captains, I should imagine.

Lieut Coyle   Now look . . .

Maryanne   One of your kin.

Lieut Coyle   I'm warning you . . .

Maryanne   Three guineas, he says.

Lieut Coyle   Don't . . .

Maryanne   I could trade three sheep off her virginity alone.

Lieut Coyle *grabs* **Maryanne** *by the hair.*

Maryanne   Now that's what we call a wager, sir.

Long pause.

Lieut Coyle   Is she on the rag?

Pause.

Maryanne . . .

Maryanne   What?

Lieut Coyle   Is she on the rag?

Maryanne   Pull it out with your teeth.

Lieut Coyle *draws his sword with his free hand.*

Lieut Coyle   Living Devil, you!

Maryanne   And may you choke on it, sir.

Lieut Coyle   I should cut your filthy tongue out!

Maryanne   Do you want me to scream?

Lieut Coyle *aims his sword at* **Maryanne**'s *face.*

Lieut Coyle Tell me where he is, damn you!

Maryanne You want me to scream, Lieutenant?

Lieut Coyle That's enough of your treachery!

Maryanne You want me to fall on my knees?

Lieut Coyle For the last time . . . !

Maryanne I'll tell you nothing.

Lieut Coyle Hand him over to me – speak!

Maryanne Unless it's my blood you're after . . .

Lieut Coyle Your blood is right, woman.

Maryanne Well, go on!

Ellen (*off*) Mammy!

Maryanne Go on, I said!

Ellen *quickly enters, pursued by* **Lieut Ryan.**

Ellen (*as she enters*) Mammy, please, I was only trying to climb the horse!

Lieut Coyle Answer me!

Ellen Tell him, Mammy, tell him!

Maryanne I'll not make a squeak, you mongrel.

Ellen He thinks I was trying to steal it, but I wasn't, I swear!

Lieut Coyle To Hell with you!

He slashes **Maryanne**'s *face.*

Ellen Mammy!

Lieut Coyle *pushes* **Maryanne** *off her stool.*

Ellen Mammy, no!

Blackout.

Three

The tavern.

Night.

The storm continues outside.

Dermot *and* **Sgt Browne, Capt Farrell, Capt Skelton,**
and **Cpl O'Connor** *are sitting at a table, with drinks.* **Dermot** *is
covered in blood, and clutching onto a dead piglet. With his other hand
he wields a blunt knife. Attached to his ankles are chains that should be
fastened together and then tied to a tree, but are unlocked, allowing him
to move freely.*

L-Cpl Finnigan *guards the tavern door. The* **Pot-Boy** *is serving
drinks. The* **Fiddler** *and the* **Piper** *play music in the corner.*

*On the wall hangs a large portrait of King George III among angels, as he
ascends to Heaven.*

Dermot   . . . and there's just him and me and we're down
on the ground and I have the little bastard by the throat. He's
wriggling and squealing like the very plague pins him down.
'No more!' he cries. 'Have mercy!'

The **Redcoats** *laugh.*

Dermot   'Spare a penny for my soul!'

Sgt Browne (*laughing*)   Pour the boy a drink!

Dermot   Boxing my head with his four trotters he was!
Lashing his tongue as if his spit would burn my very flesh –
I tell you, this was no ordinary pig!

Capt Farrell   God save us!

Dermot   I swear he might have crushed my very skull had
he the property! Had I not the will of Jesus Christ at my hand,
had I not lived to taste the sacrament!

Capt Skelton   Pity the poor beast.

Dermot   Of course I finished him.

Cpl O'Connor   You slashed him?

Dermot   I cut his very heart out!

Cpl O'Connor   From ear to ear?

Dermot   From top to stinking toe.

Capt Farrell   I don't believe it.

Dermot   As God is my witness . . .

Capt Skelton   As God is your what?

Capt Farrell   The boy couldn't crack an egg without crying to his mammy!

They laugh.

Dermot   I have him gaping like an old drunken whore, I do!

Sgt Browne (*to the* **Pot-Boy**)   Are you deaf, you fucking weasel?

Dermot (*to* **O'Connor**)   I have him begging for mercy, I tell you.

Cpl O'Connor   Do you now?

Dermot   I have him dragging his four legs through the mud and through the marshes. Of course I can barely see my own rotten body never mind the remains of this poor beast. But I keep him gripped. I keep him gripped against my hips like he's a Sheela-na-Gig, by Christ, as your very skin might hold its wound! The thunder's cracking skulls and the lightning clips my heels, but I charge and I charge till we're lost within the Vale. It's here we catch our breath and with him beating at my face, I slit him like a medlar and he tumbles to his death!

The **Redcoats** *laugh and clap.* **Sgt Browne** *kisses* **Dermot.**

Sgt Browne (*laughing*)   Give me a kiss, me boy!

Dermot   That'll teach him, won't it?

Sgt Browne (*laughing*)   Papist scum, you!

Capt Farrell (*laughing*)   You filthy bastard, Sergeant Browne!

Dermot   That'll teach him, look!

Capt Farrell   You'll bring us all down with the plague!

Sgt Browne   Fill up his beaker, damn you!

Dermot (*to* **O'Connor**)   Tell me that'll teach him though, won't it?

Cpl O'Connor (*laughing*)   Oh, it's a fine story, I'll grant you.

Sgt Browne   Fine story!

Cpl O'Connor   It does well raise a few eyebrows, Sergeant Browne.

Sgt Browne   This is the stuff of kings, my lad!

Dermot   It is?

Sgt Browne   You'll be decorated for this, I grant you!

Capt Farrell   Did he offend you?

Dermot   What?

Capt Skelton   This beast you speak of.

Capt Farrell   You must have good reason.

Cpl O'Connor   Let's pray he was no Prussian.

Capt Skelton   What had he done to you exactly?

Dermot   Done?

Capt Farrell   His crime, boy, his crime!

Cpl O'Connor   You must have killed for a reason, lad, come on.

Dermot   But I just told –

Capt Farrell (*mimics* **Dermot**)   Sodomy, by God!

They laugh.

Capt Farrell (*mimics* **Dermot**, *raising his glass*)   In the name of Our Grace!

Sgt Browne   In the name of the Pontiff!

Capt Skelton   Did he stain your noble honour?

Capt Farrell/Sgt Browne   In the name of the Pope!

More laughter – they toast and drink, filling their beakers from the **Pot-Boy**'s *jug.*

Cpl O'Connor   Get it down you, lad, get it down!

Dermot   But I don't know what you mean . . .

Sgt Browne   Finish your drink, you cold-hearted bastard!

Dermot   On my honour –

Capt Skelton   His honour – now did I not tell you?

Dermot   By the honour of the Virgin Mary –

Capt Skelton   The boy's a martyr, by Christ!

Cpl O'Connor   Was it justice you were seeking?

Dermot   What?

Sgt Browne   Should we send for the bailiffs, young sir?

Capt Farrell   Should we keep watch for when he returns?

Dermot   When who returns?

Sgt Browne (*calls*)   Send for the watch!

Dermot   No, you're not hearing me.

Sgt Browne   The watch!

Dermot   You're not hearing me, please!

Sgt Browne (*calls to the* **Pot-Boy**)   Send for the watch, lad!

Capt Farrell   There's a door here lost its hinges!

Sgt Browne   Send for the watch, I say!

Dermot   But you're not hearing me out, boys!

Cpl O'Connor   Oh, we hear you, Dermot, we hear you.

Capt Skelton   Ah, but can we trust his word?

Dermot   I tell you, I killed him!

Capt Farrell/Sgt Browne   Oh!

Dermot   I tore his stinking apple out! With me own front teeth!

Cpl O'Connor   All right, we hear you, Dermot!

Dermot   Why do you think I braved the storm?!

Capt Farrell   So you might hang off my balls?

Dermot   Why would I do that?

Cpl O'Connor   Oh, you can be sure we'll find good reason.

Dermot   I tell you, I never saw such suffering as in this foul pig!

As **Dermot** *speaks, the* **Redcoats** *fill up their drinks.*

Capt Farrell *takes* **Dermot**'s *cup and pisses in it. The cup is then passed to each* **Redcoat**, *each man spitting in it.*

Dermot   He wept and he prayed, but I wouldn't grant him penance – no, I wouldn't be his witness. They can all of them rot in Hell before I'll hand him back to Jesus, if they think I'll toss forgiveness like a beggar to a fool. The animal's mine, by God, and I'd sooner sell the Temple! I'd sooner trade the Baptist than to toil another day. To have her use me for a haywain, to have her curse me like a mule – and for what?

Capt Farrell/Sgt Browne   'For what?'

Dermot   To keep me from my liberty, to keep me from the call. To keep me from my duty, that to serve you, one and all!

The **Redcoats** *laugh.*

Dermot   It's true, I tell you!

Cpl O'Connor *(laughing)*   A soldier no less!

Capt Farrell *(laughing)*   To honour and to serve . . .

Capt Skelton (*laughing*)   Amen!

Sgt Browne (*laughing*)   Amen is right!

Cpl O'Connor (*laughing*)   Why didn't you tell us before, boy?

Sgt Browne (*laughing*)   Amen if he were to ever join my regiment!

Dermot   Let me join you, masters, please!

Capt Farrell (*laughing*)   Shall we recruit him, do you think?

Sgt Browne   On your life, Captain Farrell.

Dermot   You think I'm mad?!

Sgt Browne (*to* **Farrell**)   I'd sooner employ your bedwetting ma.

Dermot   You think I don't know?!

Capt Farrell   I think you'd better calm down.

Dermot   You think I haven't seen them?!

Capt Farrell   Now, come on, Dermot . . .

Dermot   You think I haven't seen the ships?!

Capt Skelton   Get a hold on yourself!

Dermot   You think I haven't seen them? You think I don't know what you're plotting? To keep me from my freedom, to keep me stranded on this isle. Chained like a prisoner while you sail away with Daddy – do you think I don't know?

Cpl O'Connor   Oh, we know all right.

Dermot   She told me herself, she did.

Cpl O'Connor   Oh, she did, God bless her.

Dermot   It came from her own two lips, the witch!

Sgt Browne   A witch, he claims!

Dermot   The witch my mother – don't you laugh at me!

Capt Farrell   Who's laughing?

Dermot She'd lay a curse on you in a second!

Capt Farrell Do you see me laughing, Captain Skelton?

Dermot Mother of mine with her four fiendish heads!
A monster, I grant you, a malignant maternal moan!

Capt Farrell She has how many heads?

Dermot Aye, and a fifth growing out from her hunchback!

Capt Farrell It would seem she needs a surgeon, my lad.

Dermot There's not a surgeon could contend with her foul
humours, she's a witch and nothing more! – Don't laugh, I say,
she'll have you in the mouth of Hell if you do so dare mock!

Capt Farrell (*laughs*) Oh!

Capt Skelton Are you threatening us, Dermot?

Dermot I've had a lifetime bent under her inhuman will.
If you could see what I have had to suffer! Chained and beat
like a flea-bitten rover, as though I were two balls short of a
man. Kept as a slave as though I were no better than a black
man! A foreigner who couldn't claim a sword if it struck him,
nor to even dream of being one of you proud gentlemen, and
to honour and to serve his country.

Capt Skelton Whose country?

Dermot Any but this.

Capt Skelton A traitor no less!

Dermot Why do you think I came and sought you out?!

Capt Skelton A traitor to his own fair land!

Dermot She dragged me out of the cabin she did, out of my
own home! She told me to come and find you, that I myself
might beg your service! 'Go and prove yourself a killer,
Dermot, go and find your precious daddy! Go and tell them
you want to live the life of a soldier, boy, for I'm done with
you!'

Cpl O'Connor Oh, she didn't!

Dermot   Her own son disowned!

Cpl O'Connor   This is a sorry tale.

Dermot   That I should ever call her mother of mine!

Cpl O'Connor   Let it out, son, let it out.

Dermot   She wants to see me fail, I tell you! She wants to keep him for herself and to leave me at the mercy of the storm! If you would only help me prove her wrong, if you might see my potential.

Cpl O'Connor (*to* **Browne**)   I once saw a witch in the forest, by God.

Dermot   I slaughtered them for you, look!

Sgt Browne   It's a trick, I tell you!

Dermot   But I did it all for you!

Capt Skelton   Now now, Dermot . . .

Dermot   To prove that I can kill, to prove to my daddy!

Sgt Browne   Finish your drink now, sit down.

Cpl O'Connor   You've hardly wet your lip, look.

Capt Skelton *throws his drink at* **Dermot**'s *face.*

Capt Skelton   Call yourself a man, finish your drink!

Dermot   But I can't –

Cpl O'Connor   Go on, boy!

Dermot   But you can't expect me to –

Capt Farrell   Go on, you worm!

Capt Farrell *forces the cup of piss and spit down* **Dermot**'s *throat.*

Capt Skelton   Loosen your tongue!

Farrell/O'Connor/Skelton   Drink it up! / Go on, Dermot! / Every last drop, go on! (*Etc.*)

Sgt Browne (*to the* **Pot-Boy**)   Are you going to just stand there, lad?

Sgt Browne *takes the piglet and throws it to the* **Pot-Boy**.

Sgt Browne   Tie it to the spit, go on!

The **Pot-Boy** *takes the piglet. During the following he ties it to the spit over the fire and roasts the piglet, slowly turning the spit.*

Sgt Browne (*to the* **Pot-Boy**)   That I must suffer this watered-down swill, do you want me to starve to death as well?!

The **Redcoats** *cheer as* **Dermot** *finishes his drink.*

Cpl O'Connor (*laughing*)   By Christ, you're a marvel, lad!

Sgt Browne   Marvel nothing, it's a plot!

Cpl O'Connor   But he's a killer, by God!

Sgt Browne   Killer my backside!

Cpl O'Connor   He was sent by his own dear mammy!

Sgt Browne   He couldn't hurt a bee if it stung him.

Dermot   I could cut you down to size!

Sgt Browne   Oh, really?

Dermot   I could take you down with my little finger if I be so pleased!

Sgt Browne   Is that a challenge, boy?

Dermot   I could claim you for a signet on my wedding day.

Sgt Browne (*to* **O'Connor**)   Is he challenging me, Corporal?

Dermot   Do I look like a coward to you?

Sgt Browne   Damn you to Hell!

Dermot (*strikes* **Browne**)   Well, do I?

The **Redcoats** *laugh.*

Capt Farrell (*laughs*)   Oh, he's no coward, Sergeant, I'll lay my life on that.

Dermot (*strikes* **Browne**)   Red-breasted oaf!

Sgt Browne   By Christ!

Dermot (*strikes* **Browne**)   I should use you for my –

Sgt Browne *grabs* **Dermot** *by the throat. The others laugh.*

Dermot   Aah!

Sgt Browne   Now, listen . . .

Dermot (*struggling for breath*)   Please . . .

Sgt Browne   Are you listening?

Dermot (*struggling, nods*)   I–I–I–I . . .

Again, over the dialogue, the **Redcoats** *fill up the cups with drink.*

Sgt Browne *has* **Dermot** *by the throat.*

Sgt Browne   Do you know who I am?

Dermot *struggles to speak.*

Sgt Browne   Do you see that portrait on the wall?

Dermot *struggles to speak.*

Sgt Browne   Do you not recognise your King?

Dermot *struggles to speak.*

Sgt Browne   Well, do you?

Dermot *struggles to speak.*

Sgt Browne   You think you can come here and lay claim to His Majesty's keepers? Am I no more than a pot-boy to you?

Capt Skelton   Let him go, Sergeant.

Sgt Browne   Am I and these fine fellows –

Capt Skelton   You'll break his neck you carry on.

Sgt Browne   – are we no better than the pigs you claim to fight on?

Cpl O'Connor   Come now, Sergeant Browne, don't –

Sgt Browne Well?!

Sgt Browne *slams* **Dermot***'s head on the table.*

Dermot (*gasping for breath*)   No!

Sgt Browne Have you come to taunt us, soldier?

Dermot (*gasping*)   Please . . .

Sgt Browne Have you come to taunt us?

Dermot (*gasping*)   Please, I beg you . . .

Sgt Browne Come to taunt us on the eve of battle. The last night in our own fair country, the land that bore us.

Dermot (*gasping*)   I only want to –

Sgt Browne Are we not allowed some celebration?

Dermot (*gasping*)   Of course, of course –

Sgt Browne A time to grieve at least?

Dermot (*gasping*)   I deny you nothing, sir.

Sgt Browne Can I not share a drink with these noble men for whom I'd wage my own life?

Dermot (*gasping*)   You can drink all you like!

Capt Skelton Murdering swine, you.

Dermot What?

Capt Skelton Murdering cunt.

Dermot But I only want –

Sgt Browne Come to ruin our party.

Cpl O'Connor We should gut the stinking wretch.

Dermot But I only want to help!

Cpl O'Connor I should toast his kidneys for me horse.

Sgt Browne I'll toast to that!

Dermot Let me fight your honourable cause!

Cpl O'Connor Honourable cause.

Sgt Browne I'll toast the kidneys, the horse and its mare, by Christ, my soul's already damned!

Capt Skelton And whom should we fight, Dermot?

Dermot The French!

Capt Farrell Oh, the French!

Dermot We fight the French, sir! We fight for the Commonwealth, we do! We fight for the wealth and rights of every living Englishman!

Capt Skelton Do you bewitch us, Dermot?

Dermot Bewitch? No, of course not!

Capt Farrell On your feet.

Dermot But it's true, boys, I swear my life on it!

Capt Farrell On your feet, come on!

Capt Farrell *slams his sword on the table. The other* **Redcoats** *cheer.*

Capt Farrell Give me your sword, O'Connor.

Sgt Browne On your feet, you heard the man!

Dermot But haven't I proved myself enough?

Sgt Browne/Cpl O'Connor On your feet!

Dermot *is pulled to his feet by* **Sgt Browne** *and* **Cpl O'Connor**.

Sgt Browne And so Lazarus arose.

Dermot No . . .

Capt Farrell At arms, boy!

Dermot No, please, you're hurting me.

During the following **Capt Farrell** *takes* **Cpl O'Connor***'s sword.* **Sgt Browne** *gives* **Dermot** *the sword from the table.*

Capt Farrell Threaten your betters?

Dermot   But I've already shown you.

Capt Farrell   In the presence of our monarch!

Cpl O'Connor   Go for his belly, Dermot, go on.

Dermot   Please, don't –

Sgt Browne   Go for his throat, lad!

Capt Skelton   Perhaps he doesn't want to fight.

Cpl O'Connor   He doesn't stand a chance, the skin-and-boned bastard, go on.

Capt Farrell   Strike me!

Dermot   What?

Cpl O'Connor   Aim for his chest!

Capt Skelton   Perhaps he'd rather settle the matter with a round of cards.

Capt Farrell   Strike me, go on!

Capt Farrell *deals a few blows at* **Dermot***, who dodges away.*

The others laugh.

Capt Farrell   Strike me!

Dermot   But I haven't –

Capt Farrell   Go on!

Redcoats   Go on, Dermot! / His head, his head! / Hold it upright, you fool! (*Etc.*)

Capt Farrell   Are you a killer or not?

Dermot   You're not giving me a chance!

Sgt Browne   Draw your sword!

Dermot   Can we not just finish our drinks?

Skelton/Browne/O'Connor   Draw your sword!

Capt Farrell   You fucking ape, you!

He advances at **Dermot**.

Dermot *deals a pathetic blow, and instantly cowers. The* **Redcoats** *cheer.*

Capt Farrell   Is that the best you can do?

Dermot   I'm sorry, I'm sorry . . .

Capt Farrell   Is that it, you fucking infant?!

Dermot   But you're not giving me a chance.

Capt Farrell   You toddler, Dermot, what?

He again charges at **Dermot**. *They fight.*

The **Redcoats** *cheer, laugh, taunt, etc.*

Sgt Browne (*laughing, drawing his sword*)   A guinea for the first man takes his fingers!

Capt Skelton (*laughing, drawing sword*)   A guinea for his eyes!

Capt Skelton *and* **Sgt Browne** *join* **Capt Farrell** *in attacking* **Dermot**.

Dermot   God save me, help!

They all fight.

Cpl O'Connor *moves to the* **Fiddler** *and the* **Piper**, *and accompanies them, clapping his hands, stamping his foot and singing.*

During the fight, **Lieut Coyle**, *followed by* **Lieut Ryan**, *enter the tavern.*

Lieut Coyle *motions to* **Lieut Ryan** *and they sit at a table, away from the others – unseen by* **Dermot**. *The* **Pot-Boy**, *who has been roasting the piglet on the spit, moves to* **Lieuts Coyle** *and* **Ryan**, *serving them drinks.*

Cpl O'Connor (*sings*)
   The corn was springing fresh and green,
   And the lark sang loud and high,
   And the red was on your lip, Mary,
   The love light in your eye.

They say there's bread and work for all,
And the sun shines always there:
But I'll not forget old Ireland,
Were it fifty times as fair.

O'Connor/Fiddler/Piper (*sing*)
No, I'll not forget old Ireland,
Were it fifty times as . . . !

Sgt Browne *feigns being hit by* **Dermot** *and falls.*

Sgt Browne (*falls*)   Aaah!

Capt Farrell   Sergeant Browne, sir!

Sgt Browne   My leg!

Over the following, **Dermot** *tries to escape, but is caught by* **L-Cpl Finnigan,** *who drags him back to* **Capt Skelton.** **Capt Farrell** *attends to* **Sgt Browne.**

Capt Farrell   Are you all right?

Sgt Browne   By Christ . . .

Capt Farrell   Are you hit, Sergeant?!

Cpl O'Connor (*to the* **Fiddler**)   You play like you were scratching your hole.

Sgt Browne   He hit me in the leg, the little bastard!

Dermot   I never touched him!

Capt Skelton (*to* **Dermot**)   Stay where you are.

Cpl O'Connor (*to the* **Fiddler**)   There's a man here dying, do you wish to finish him off?

Capt Farrell   Can you walk?

Sgt Browne   May God preserve me!

Capt Farrell   Can you walk, Sergeant?

Sgt Browne (*tries to walk*)   Aaah!

Capt Farrell   He's crippled, look!

Sgt Browne My leg, my leg!

Capt Skelton Do you see what you've done?

Sgt Browne Send for the gravedigger!

Cpl O'Connor Let me help you, Sergeant, come on.

Sgt Browne My last rites, O'Connor, I beg you.

Capt Skelton Do you see the damage you've caused?

Dermot Damage? But I didn't even come close –

Capt Skelton Is this how you repay us our kindness, boy?

Capt Farrell Bring him here.

Dermot I hardly scratched him, look!

Capt Farrell Bring him over, Captain.

Dermot He's lying to you – please!

Capt Skelton and **L-Cpl Finnigan** *pull* **Dermot** *over towards* **Capt Farrell**, *who is at the table.*

Cpl O'Connor *tends to* **Sgt Browne**.

Lieuts Coyle *and* **Ryan** *continue drinking silently at their table.*

Dermot I could hardly place my own shadow!

Capt Farrell Look at him.

Dermot There are five against one here, you can't expect me to –

Capt Farrell Take a good look.

Capt Skelton Is it your pleasure to murder members of His Majesty's armed forces?

Dermot What?

Capt Skelton Is it your will and intention to murder members of – ?

Dermot I never touched him!

Capt Farrell   Did they send you?

Dermot   Who?

Capt Farrell *strikes* **Dermot.**

Capt Farrell   Traitor!

Capt Skelton *strikes* **Dermot.**

Capt Skelton   Catholic bastard, they sent you, didn't they?

Dermot   Who?

Capt Farrell   The whiteshirts!

Dermot   What whiteshirts?

Capt Skelton   Sent to violate Brown Bess.

Dermot   But I don't know any –

Capt Farrell   We should burn him at the stake.

Sgt Browne   Take his poisonous tongue out!

Capt Farrell   Damned insurgent, you!

Sgt Browne   Bring me his tongue and he can lick my
wound!

Capt Skelton   Who sent you?

Dermot   Boys, please . . .

Sgt Browne (*to the* **Pot-Boy**)   Bring me a drink, you ape!

Capt Skelton   Who sent you?

Sgt Browne (*to the* **Pot-Boy**)   Leave that damn pig alone!

Over the following, the **Pot-Boy,** *who has returned to the spit and begun
removing the piglet, quickly dumps it on the table and pours a drink for*
Sgt Browne.

Capt Skelton   Who sent you?

Capt Farrell   Was it the Whiteshirts?

Capt Skelton   Give me their names!

Dermot What whiteshirts?

Capt Skelton Their names!

Dermot But I don't know who you mean!

Capt Skelton Tell us about your man!

Dermot I don't know any whiteshirts!

Capt Skelton Tell us about your benefactor!

Capt Farrell Was he a man or a fish?

Capt Skelton I'll wager he was neither.

Sgt Browne A guinea for your bet!

Capt Skelton Are you mocking us?

Dermot But I told you already –

Capt Farrell Was he human?

Dermot Human?

Capt Skelton Did he go by a name?

Capt Farrell Was he a man?

Dermot Yes!

Capt Farrell Was he a man?

Dermot Yes!

Capt Farrell Was he a tall man?

Dermot Who?

Capt Farrell *strikes* **Dermot**.

Dermot I don't know, sir!

Capt Farrell What?

Dermot Yes!

Capt Farrell What was he?

Dermot He was the tallest man I ever did see!

They laugh.

But he was!

Capt Skelton   Are you certain?

Dermot   I swear to you!

Sgt Browne   God help you, child!

Dermot   He was ten foot tall and climbing if he was any man at all!

They laugh.

Capt Skelton (*affects English accent*)   Oh, I expect he was a very giant, Your Honour.

Sgt Browne (*laughing*)   He'd crush you with his bare arse, he would!

Dermot   He would!

Cpl O'Connor   Oh, I doubt he was mortal at all.

Capt Farrell   Was he not one of Satan's creatures, I wonder?

Capt Skelton   Did you get a good look at his face?

Dermot   His face?

Capt Farrell   What colour was he, boy?

Dermot   Which colour would you like?

Capt Farrell *slaps* **Dermot**.

Capt Farrell   What colour was he?

Cpl O'Connor   He doesn't sound like anyone I know.

Capt Farrell   Was he a foreigner?

Dermot   If you want.

Capt Skelton   Answer the man.

Dermot   But did I not just – ?

Capt Skelton *slaps* **Dermot**.

Capt Farrell   Was he a black man?

Capt Skelton   Was he the colour of shit?

Cpl O'Connor   Did he crawl from out your hole?

Dermot   But I don't understand . . .

Sgt Browne   A soldier, he claims!

Dermot   I'm here, aren't I?

Sgt Browne   Fine soldiery to strike at his own kind!

Dermot   I'm here, look!

Capt Skelton   Oh, you're here all right.

Dermot   Just tell me what you want and I will give it to you!

Capt Skelton   You're one of us now, Dermot.

Dermot   I give you my pig!

Sgt Browne   Jesus Christ, lad . . .

Dermot   I give you my pig, I give you my pig!

Dermot *breaks free from* **Capts Skelton** *and* **Farrell***, grabbing the roasted piglet from off the table − it is very hot.*

They laugh.

Dermot   I give it to you, sir, please!

The **Pot-Boy** *tries to retrieve the piglet.*

Dermot   Let go of me!

Dermot *and the* **Pot-Boy** *wrestle over the piglet, the* **Redcoats** *laughing.*

Dermot   Get your hands off me!

Dermot *boots and beats the* **Pot-Boy** *to the ground − the* **Redcoats** *cheer.*

Dermot   I killed it for you, look!

L-Cpl Finnigan *seizes* **Dermot***, who clutches onto the piglet.*

Dermot   By my own free will!

Capt Farrell   Free will!

Dermot   It's true, I beg you!

Capt Farrell   You were captured by my own guard – free will!

Dermot   It was I who found you!

Capt Farrell   Did you not apprehend him, Finnigan?

L-Cpl Finnigan (*clutching* **Dermot**)   That's right, sir, yes.

Dermot (*struggles*)   He's lying!

L-Cpl Finnigan   He was hiding in the pigpen as you see him now. Him and his wee dagger hidden in the swill.

Dermot (*struggles*)   No, that's not it at all!

L-Cpl Finnigan   A coward if I ever saw one.

Dermot   But I meant for you to come, it was my very will and intention to do so!

Sgt Browne   A likely story.

Dermot   Just give me your orders and I will obey!

Sgt Browne   Said the fox to the hen.

Dermot   Let me prove it to you, please!

Dermot *breaks free from* **L-Cpl Finnigan** *and falls on his knees before* **Sgt Browne**.

Dermot   Let me serve my lord and master, let me serve your honest King! It's the girl you're after having, it's my pretty little sister, not me! She conspired with my mammy to unshackle me so free! I swear they'd rob the Virgin's womb if a profit it would bring!

Capt Skelton (*to* **Browne**)   He'd claim you for his wife, Browne.

Capt Farrell   Oh, they'd make a bountiful brood, by God.

Dermot (*to* **Browne**)   Don't let them leave me here.

Cpl O'Connor   Send them to the chapel!

Sgt Browne   For God's sake, will you not yield?

Dermot (*to* **Browne**)   I was a man once, please, look at me.

Sgt Browne   Get up.

Dermot (*to* **Browne**)   I was a man just like you.

Sgt Browne   Get up.

Dermot (*to* **Browne**)   You believe me though, don't you?

Sgt Browne   Get up, you mole.

Dermot   But, sir –

Sgt Browne   Embarrass me in front of my brothers.

Dermot   I'll kiss your feet.

Sgt Browne   What?

Dermot   I kiss your feet, sir!

Dermot *kisses* **Sgt Browne**'s *feet.*

Sgt Browne   Jesus Christ!

The others laugh.

Have you no shame, boy?!

He boots **Dermot** *away.*

Sgt Browne (*to* **Finnigan**)   Take him away, would you?

Dermot (*to* **Browne**)   You believe me though, don't you?

Sgt Browne   Send him back to Rome!

Dermot   But, sir, you have to –

Sgt Browne   Papist scum!

Dermot   You have to believe me.

Sgt Browne   I don't have to do anything, boy. (*To* **Finnigan**.) Take him away I said!

Dermot (*sees* **Coyle**)   You believe me, don't you, Daddy?

Capt Farrell (*laughs*)   What?

Dermot   Daddy, please, you have to tell them.

Dermot *kneels at* **Lieut Coyle**'s *feet.*

Capt Farrell (*laughs*)   Am I hearing things, Skelton?

Dermot (*to* **Coyle**)   Tell them I'm no –

Lieut Coyle *pushes* **Dermot** *away.*

Lieut Coyle   Move.

Dermot   Tell them I'm no traitor.

Lieut Coyle (*pushes* **Dermot**)   Go home.

Dermot   Tell them how I only wish to serve the greater good.

Lieut Coyle   For Christ's sake . . . !

Dermot   Father, please . . .

Lieut Coyle   Go home, I said!

He hurls **Dermot** *away.*

Long pause.

Dermot   Daddy . . .

Lieut Coyle   Let a man finish his drink, would you?

Dermot   You have to tell them, please!

Lieut Coyle (*to* **Ryan**)   Pass me that jug there, would you, Ryan?

Dermot   But I killed a pig for you.

Lieut Coyle (*grabs the ale jug himself*)   For God's sake, man!

Dermot   I went to the farm, look.

Dermot *offers the roasted piglet to* **Lieut Coyle**.

Dermot   I killed a pig for you, Daddy.

Lieut Coyle   Get that thing away from me! Jesus Christ . . .

Dermot   You remember the old farm.

Lieut Coyle   I don't know what you're talking about!

Dermot   The farm they stole from us, Daddy – please.

Sgt Browne (*grabs* **Dermot**)   All right now, that's enough.

Dermot   You remember the prayers we made.

Sgt Browne (*pulls* **Dermot** *away from* **Coyle**)   Leave the man alone!

Dermot   'For in thee, O Lord, do I put my trust!'

Sgt Browne   Enough, I say!

Sgt Browne *and* **Dermot** *struggle, as* **Dermot** *tries to fight his way back to* **Lieut Coyle**'s *table.*

Dermot (*struggles*)   'Let me never be put to confusion! Deliver me in thy righteousness and cause me to – '

Capt Skelton (*strikes* **Dermot**)   Let him finish his drink, you bairn.

Dermot   'And cause me to escape!'

Capt Farrell (*strikes* **Dermot**)   You'll have to excuse the boy, Lieutenant.

Dermot   That is what you taught me! . . .

Capt Farrell   He's out of his wits from the ale.

Dermot   Tell me you haven't forgotten, tell me that! Tell them what I'm made of at least! – What, have you lost your senses?

Sgt Browne (*strikes* **Dermot**)   Watch your manners, Whiteshirt!

Dermot (*to* **Browne**)   But I've proved I can kill, I've shown you proof already!

Capt Skelton   You've certainly done that, lad.

Capt Farrell He'd have us all spitting soil if he could.

Capt Skelton What do you say, Coyle?

Dermot Daddy, please . . .

Capt Farrell Leave the man alone!

Dermot Don't let them do this to me!

Capt Farrell *pulls* **Dermot** *away from* **Lieut Coyle**.

Capt Skelton Well, what do you say? Come on now . . .

Dermot After all you bid me promise.

Capt Farrell Be quiet!

Capt Skelton Do you not promise him a place in the regiment?

Dermot After all the years at your service –

Capt Farrell Be quiet, I say!

He strikes **Dermot.**

Capt Skelton Do you not promise him a place in the regiment?

Lieut Coyle No.

Sgt Browne Is he not your kin?

Lieut Coyle I've never seen him before.

Capt Skelton Is he not your kin, Lieutenant?

Pause.

Lieutenant . . .

Lieut Coyle No.

Sgt Browne Does he lie to us?

Lieut Coyle He's nothing.

Capt Skelton Are you certain?

Lieut Coyle He's nothing, I say! – Dear God, Skelton!

Capt Skelton   What did I tell you?

Dermot   But I swear to you, no!

Lieut Coyle   Do I have to grovel at your fucking feet?

Capt Skelton   Treachery.

Dermot   I swear to you, on my life I do!.

Capt Farrell   Stop your noise.

Dermot   You don't mean that!

Capt Farrell   That's enough!

Dermot   He doesn't mean that.

Cpl O'Connor   Oh come now, Dermot –

Dermot   He doesn't mean that, look!

Cpl O'Connor   The Lieutenant makes no claims on you.

Dermot   Look into his eyes!

Cpl O'Connor   Now if you want us to be merciful . . .

Sgt Browne   Merciful my two balls!

Dermot   But I know he doesn't.

Sgt Browne   Finish the bastard!

Dermot   He doesn't mean what he says, he wouldn't do that to me.

Sgt Browne   Take his head off, Captain!

Dermot   His only living son, he wouldn't –

Cpl O'Connor   His head, his head!

Dermot   He wouldn't let that happen! Daddy, no!

Lieut Coyle   All right now, just –

Sgt Browne   Take it off, for the love of God, take it off!

Dermot *faints.*

Sgt Browne   I'm sick of hearing him squeal!

He grabs **Dermot** *and draws his sword.*

Sgt Browne   Dirty heathen bastard, you.

Lieut Coyle   That's enough now, Sergeant!

Sgt Browne   Try to infiltrate our honest −

Lieut Coyle   That's enough, I beg you − stop!

Lieut Coyle *comes between* **Sgt Browne** *and* **Dermot***, drawing his sword.*

Pause.

Lieut Coyle   Jesus Christ, Browne . . .

Sgt Browne   Put down your weapon, sir.

Lieut Coyle   Have you not punished the boy enough?

Sgt Browne   Put it down.

Lieut Coyle   Can't you see he meant no harm?

Sgt Browne   Threaten me with your blunt metal!

He strikes **Lieut Coyle***'s sword away.*

Capt Farrell   All right now, boys . . .

Sgt Browne   What are you?!

Pause.

Lieut Coyle   Look . . .

Sgt Browne   What are you, Coyle?!

Sgt Browne *strikes* **Lieut Coyle***'s sword.*

Lieut Coyle   Just let me talk to him.

Sgt Browne   Are you his fucking pimp that you stand in the way of your own brothers?!

Sgt Browne *strikes at* **Lieut Coyle** *a couple of times,* **Lieut Coyle** *blocking him.*

Capt Farrell   Steady on now, Browne.

Sgt Browne   Are you his pimp, sir?!

Lieut Coyle   Forgive me, just –

Capt Skelton   Perhaps you'd care for us to step aside, sir, no?

Lieut Coyle   He's not worth such trouble – Captain, please.

Capt Farrell   Would you like some privacy?

Lieut Coyle   I'm certain he didn't mean to harm anyone . . .

Sgt Browne   He's a traitor, Lieutenant!

Lieut Coyle   He needs a doctor, that's all.

Sgt Browne   He needs what?

Lieut Coyle   Just let me speak with him a minute, Sergeant.

Sgt Browne   The end of my sword!

Lieut Coyle   But I can prove it . . .

Sgt Browne   The gaol, Lieutenant!

Lieut Coyle   Let me prove it to you, damn it!

He strikes **Sgt Browne**'s *sword away with his own.*

Cpl O'Connor   Oh come now, Coyle, we were only having a little fun with the boy.

Lieut Coyle   Dermot, please . . .

Capt Farrell (*to the* **Pot-Boy**)   A round of drinks here, lad!

Lieut Coyle   Come on now, child, get up off the floor.

He crouches down by the unconscious **Dermot.**

Sgt Browne   Jesus save us!

Lieut Coyle   Get up, Dermot, come on.

Sgt Browne (*to* **Skelton**)   Are you just going to stand there?

Lieut Coyle   For God's sake, wake up!

Cpl O'Connor I think we found our answer, Browne.

Lieut Coyle Wake up, I say!

Capt Skelton He needs a doctor all right.

Lieut Coyle Dermot, please . . .

Sgt Browne I can stand this no more.

Lieut Coyle Don't make a fool of me now!

Sgt Browne *pulls* **Lieut Coyle** *away from* **Dermot**.

Sgt Browne Pull yourself together, Coyle!

Lieut Coyle Don't do this, child!

Sgt Browne On your feet now, be a man!

Lieut Coyle For Christ's sake, Browne –

Capt Farrell Let him go.

Lieut Coyle – can you not think without your fists for one minute?!

Capt Farrell Behave yourselves, the pair of you!

Lieut Coyle Captain Farrell, please . . .

Capt Farrell At ease, Lieutenant.

Lieut Coyle But I only –

Capt Farrell At ease!

Lieut Coyle But if you would just give me one moment –

Capt Farrell Do you want to shame the whole regiment?

Lieut Coyle But I only want you to think twice before –

Sgt Browne The boy's a traitor!

Lieut Coyle You don't know that, Sergeant.

Sgt Browne It came from his own two lips!

Lieut Coyle Captain Farrell, come on now!

Sgt Browne   I know what I heard!

Lieut Coyle   You know that if we might just speak reasonably . . .

Sgt Browne   Reasonably he says!

Cpl O'Connor   Wake up, you toad, you heard the man!

He kicks the unconscious **Dermot**

Lieut Coyle   Jesus Christ, don't –

Cpl O'Connor   Explain yourself!

He kicks **Dermot**

Lieut Coyle   O'Connor, don't –

Sgt Browne   On your feet, traitor!

He boots **Dermot**

Lieut Coyle   Would you please stop . . . ?!

Sgt Browne *and* **Cpl O'Connor** *boot* **Dermot**

Lieut Coyle   Stop this madness! Tell them to stop, Captain!

Capt Skelton   Can you vouch for him?

Lieut Coyle   Let him stand trial at least!

Capt Skelton   Then you would speak for him, Lieutenant.

Capt Farrell   You think he's innocent.

Lieut Coyle   I hardly know the boy!

Capt Skelton   And your defence?

Long pause.

And your defence?

Lieut Coyle   Look . . .

Capt Farrell   Speak up, Coyle.

Lieut Coyle   He's no threat to any one of us, Captain.

Cpl O'Connor   So you do know him?

Lieut Coyle   He's an animal, he should never have set foot in this place.

Sgt Browne   Did you lie to us?

Lieut Coyle   Of course not!

Sgt Browne   Did he not lie, Corporal?

Lieut Coyle   I only meant . . .

Capt Farrell   You don't sound too sure.

Lieut Coyle   I know him from the town, sir, that's all! Surely you must have seen him yourselves?

Capt Skelton   Have you seen him, Farrell?

Lieut Coyle   I've seen him hiding out in the forest, Captain, he's a scavenger, that's all. He's lived here all his life, he doesn't know right from wrong, it's his breeding.

Capt Farrell   He seems to know you, sir.

Lieut Coyle   He has me mistaken.

Capt Farrell   Did you not apprehend him then?

Lieut Coyle   What?

Capt Skelton   In the forest.

Lieut Coyle   I think it was the forest.

Capt Skelton   You let him go?

Lieut Coyle   I don't remember –

Capt Skelton   You just said so, Coyle! In the forest!

Capt Farrell   When in the forest?

Lieut Coyle   Don't make me repeat myself, Captain Farrell. I just told you, he's an idiot.

Capt Farrell   Answer the question!

Lieut Coyle   A harmless idiot – what good would a trial do? Yes, I pitied him! I pitied him as I would a stray dog, wouldn't you also? So I gave him a little meat from my plate, so what?! The boy obviously has no family to speak of – For all I know he might come from any of your noble blood.

Capt Skelton   But it's you he calls Father.

Lieut Coyle   He'd give a rat the same title, come on with you!

Capt Farrell   And the witch?

Sgt Browne   The witch is his mistress, I warrant.

Lieut Coyle   The witch is his own brain!

Capt Skelton (*laughs*)   It's his what now?

Lieut Coyle   His brain, Captain Skelton, you know what I mean! It's the product of his breeding.

Capt Farrell   But you swore he had no such thing.

Lieut Coyle   I swore nothing of the sort! For God's sake, Ryan, will you not speak?!

He marches over to **Lieut Ryan***, who remains seated.*

Lieut Coyle   Speak up, damn you!

Lieut Ryan   But, sir –

Lieut Coyle *strikes* **Lieut Ryan**.

Lieut Coyle   Dumb bastard, what have I taught you?

Capt Skelton   Now, Coyle . . .

Lieut Coyle   Tell them I'm no hypocrite – speak up!

Capt Skelton   That's enough now, don't –

Lieut Coyle   What have I taught you, boy?!

Lieut Ryan   I can't say, sir, I –

Lieut Coyle   What have I taught you?! – Come on!

Cpl O'Connor   Do you have something to tell us, Ryan?

Lieut Coyle   Come on now, will you not defend your master?

Cpl O'Connor   Well?

Lieut Coyle   Don't just sit there – haven't we served together long enough?

Capt Skelton   Let him speak for himself, Coyle.

Cpl O'Connor   Would you defend him?

Lieut Coyle (*to* **Ryan**)   If it's your uncle you're worried about –

Capt Farrell   Lieutenant Ryan!

Lieut Ryan   No, sir.

Capt Farrell   Does he tell us the truth?

Lieut Ryan   He does not, sir, no! He's a liar and a traitor!

Sgt Browne (*laughs*)   Oh!

Lieut Ryan   I've seen him with my own two eyes!

Lieut Coyle   God help you, boy.

Lieut Ryan   Him and the witch, sir, on my honour!

Sgt Browne (*laughs*)   Honour, indeed!

Lieut Ryan   They do lie like lovers in the forest!

Lieut Coyle   God help you to your death.

Cpl O'Connor (*to* **Ryan**)   Oh, that takes some balls, lad, go on with you!

Lieut Coyle   God help you, you ungrateful little bastard!

Lieut Coyle *goes for* **Lieut Ryan.**

Lieut Ryan   Don't you touch me!

Lieut Coyle   I swear on your unborn children!

Capt Farrell   You swear nothing, Coyle!

He seizes **Lieut Coyle**.

Lieut Coyle   They'll finish you, spoiled brat! You decoration you!

Capt Farrell   That's an order!

Lieut Coyle   You won't last a second in that war!

Capt Farrell *strikes* **Lieut Coyle**.

Lieut Coyle   Aah!

Capt Farrell   That's an order, Coyle – let him go!

Sgt Browne (*to the* **Pot-Boy**)   You there!

Capt Farrell (*to* **Coyle**)   If you so much as mark this boy . . .

Lieut Coyle   He is my responsibility!

Cpl O'Connor (*to the* **Pot-Boy**)   Fill up his booze, lad, go on!

Sgt Browne (*to the* **Pot-Boy**)   Go on with you, hurry!

Capt Skelton (*to* **Finnigan**, *of* **Dermot**)   Mop up this beast, would you, Finnigan?

Cpl O'Connor (*hands* **Ryan** *a pipe*)   Have my pipe – that's it, put your feet up!

Capt Farrell (*to* **Coyle**)   Don't struggle with me now, Coyle, you've been named.

Lieut Coyle   Jesus Christ, Farrell, can't you see he's – ?

Capt Farrell *strikes* **Lieut Coyle**.

Capt Farrell   Shut your mouth!

Lieut Coyle   Can't you see he's frightened out his wits? He'll say anything –

Capt Farrell   He'll speak before the Colonel – stay down!

Lieut Coyle   How long have we known each other, eh?

Sgt Browne   Not long enough, it seems!

Lieut Coyle   But, Sergeant Browne, you know that I would never –

Sgt Browne   Lying dog!

He winds **Lieut Coyle**.

Lieut Coyle   Ooh!

Sgt Browne   You and your dirty pigling!

Capt Skelton (*to* **Finnigan**)   Take him to the gaol, man, go on!

Capt Farrell (*to* **Finnigan**)   Take his eyes out, you hear?!

L-Cpl Finnigan *takes* **Dermot***, who is beginning to wake, by his legs and proceeds to drag him to the exit.*

Lieut Coyle   But, Captain, please, you really don't have to do this . . .

Dermot (*waking, to* **Finnigan**)   Let go of me, oh!

Capt Skelton   Let him wake the beggar blind!

Cpl O'Connor   Can we not have some music here, you scum?

Cpl O'Connor *strikes the* **Fiddler** *and* **Piper** *who begin to play.*

Dermot (*struggles*)   Let go of me, I said!

Lieut Coyle   He's just a boy, please . . .

Dermot (*struggles*)   Let go! Oh, help, help!

Dermot *struggles as* **L-Cpl Finnigan** *tries to drag him out.*

Dermot   Daddy, save me!

Lieut Coyle   He's just a boy for Christ's sake! For Christ's sake, will you not . . . ?!

Lieut Coyle *breaks free from* **Capt Farrell** *and attacks the* **Redcoats** *with his sword.*

Capt Farrell   Seize him!

Lieut Coyle *and the* **Redcoats** *fight.*

Capt Farrell Seize him, Corporal!

Lieut Coyle Run away, Dermot, run!

Dermot *grabs the piglet and exits, charging out of the cabin. He is pursued by* **L-Cpl Finnigan**, *who also exits.*

The others fight.

During the fight, the **Pot-Boy** *is accidently hit by a sword.*

Over the rest of the scene, the **Pot-Boy** *is left to die, blood pouring from his wound.*

Capt Skelton Take him down, Sergeant!

Capt Farrell Hit him in the gut!

Capt Skelton Take him down!

Capt Farrell The gut, his guts!

Sgt Browne Treacherous old fool!

The **Redcoats** *knock* **Lieut Coyle**'s *sword out of his hands and push him to the ground.*

Lieut Coyle Aaaah!

Capt Farrell Hold him down!

Lieut Coyle *tries to break free.*

Capt Farrell Hold him down, Corporal, move!

Over the following, **Cpl O'Connor**, **Capt Skelton** *and* **Sgt Browne** *pin* **Lieut Coyle** *to one of the chairs.*

Lieut Coyle For Christ's sake, show some mercy!

Sgt Browne And whose mercy is that, Coyle?

Lieut Coyle Are we not of the same stuff?

Sgt Browne The mercy of your Pope?

Lieut Coyle We are made of the same blood, Captain!

Capt Skelton   But I thought you'd never met the boy!

Sgt Browne   They're star-crossed lovers, by Jove!

Lieut Coyle   You know what I mean, damn you!

Cpl O'Connor (*laughs, to the musicians*)   A ballad for his holiness! A ballad, a ballad! Soften your bow!

Pot-Boy   May the Devil fuck you all!

Lieut Coyle   We are all of us made of the same flesh and blood, you know that!

Capt Farrell   Oh, we are?

Lieut Coyle   You know that, sir!

Capt Skelton   Hold him down, Corporal.

Lieut Coyle   All of you fucking hypocrites . . .

Pot-Boy   May he fuck your mothers all!

The **Redcoats** *struggle to keep* **Lieut Coyle** *down on his seat.*

Sgt Browne   Stay down!

Lieut Coyle   You were all of you born Catholic – do you think I don't know that? Every last one of you! You only converted out of fear, for all I know you still practise it to this day!

Capt Farrell   Hold your tongue!

He strikes **Lieut Coyle** *across the face with his cup.*

Lieut Coyle   Aah!

Capt Farrell   Hold your tongue unless it's a confession you do speak.

Capt Skelton   Take his legs, Sergeant.

Sgt Browne (*moves to* **Coyle**)   Dirty vermin, you.

Capt Skelton   Draw the blood to his head, go on.

Sgt Browne   Make a mockery of our trust!

Over the next, **Cpl O'Connor** *and* **Sgt Browne** *pull a struggling* **Lieut Coyle** *by his feet, and hang him upside down.*

Lieut Coyle   No, please!

Capt Farrell   Don't struggle now, boy!

Lieut Coyle   Please, don't do this!

Capt Skelton   Lift him up, I said!

Lieut Coyle   But I swear to you, boys, I swear!

Cpl O'Connor   Does he swear, do you think?

Lieut Coyle   You're making a terrible mistake, on my life! As God is my witness, I swear to you, I would never betray you!

Lieut Coyle, *upside down, is kicked in the head by* **Capt Skelton**.

Capt Skelton   Swear to the King of England!

Lieut Coyle   The King of England!

Capt Skelton   Swear it!

He kicks **Lieut Coyle** *in the head.*

Capt Farrell   Are you lying to us again? He's lying to us again!

Capt Skelton   Lieutenant Coyle!

Lieut Coyle   I swear!

Capt Farrell   He's all gas, look!

Capt Skelton   Are you prepared to die for your King?

Pause.

Lieutenant Thomas Coyle . . .

Capt Farrell   Answer the man!

Capt Skelton   Are you prepared to die for your King?

Lieut Coyle   You know I am!

Capt Skelton   Call yourself a soldier.

Lieut Coyle Jesus Christ . . .

Capt Skelton *strikes* **Lieut Coyle** *across the face.*

Lieut Coyle Aah!

Capt Skelton Speak!

Capt Farrell Catholic worm, you.

Cpl O'Connor Answer the question.

Capt Skelton *strikes* **Lieut Coyle** *twice about the face.*

Lieut Coyle I am!

Capt Skelton Are you prepared to die −

Lieut Coyle I am!

Capt Skelton − for your King?

Lieut Coyle I am, I am!

Cpl O'Connor *and* **Sgt Browne** *throw* **Lieut Coyle** *to the ground − crash.*

Lieut Coyle Aaaahh!

The **Redcoats** *laugh.*

Lieut Coyle Are you trying to fucking cripple me too?

Sgt Browne Is that shit coming off him?

Cpl O'Connor He's soiled himself, look!

Sgt Browne God save us, Captain Farrell!

Capt Farrell We should get him out of these clothes then, boys!

Capt Farrell *grabs* **Lieut Coyle**.

Lieut Coyle No! No, wait, please!!

Lieut Coyle, *struggling, has his uniform ripped off him by the* **Redcoats**, *leaving him in just his undergarments.*

Lieut Coyle Please, stop!

Capt Skelton   On your feet!

Lieut Coyle   Stop this madness! I promise you I'll –

Sgt Browne   On your fucking feet!

Lieut Coyle   I'll die for you, I promise!

The **Redcoats** *pull* **Lieut Coyle**, *in just his undergarments, to his feet. On his throat hangs a silver chain, off which hangs the crucifix.*

Sgt Browne   I think we found our answer, boys!

Lieut Coyle   I promise you, dear God! Dear God, I would never –

Sgt Browne *rips off the chain/crucifix.*

Lieut Coyle   Agh!

Sgt Browne   The King of the Jews no less!

Capt Farrell   And the meek shall inherit the Earth!

He rummages through **Lieut Coyle**'s *uniform.*

Cpl O'Connor   God help you, Coyle. You must know you're forbidden to wear such tokens.

Lieut Coyle   It isn't mine.

Capt Skelton   You violate the law.

Lieut Coyle   It was given to me – I beg you.

Capt Skelton   What?

Lieut Coyle   I forgot I even had the damn thing.

Capt Skelton   And did one of your allies give you this?

Cpl O'Connor   Surely you know better than to wear it on your person?

Capt Farrell *discovers the missal.*

Lieut Coyle   But I wasn't –

Capt Farrell   The man's armed, I warrant!

Sgt Browne   The man's a fool!

Capt Farrell   For my sins, that he would carry a prayer book too!

Lieut Coyle   But I was only holding them for someone.

Capt Skelton   Someone who?

Lieut Coyle   They don't belong to me, they're not −

Capt Skelton   Someone who, Lieutenant? A priest?

Cpl O'Connor   A Jesuit, I warrant.

Capt Farrell   Would you like to hear a passage, Coyle?

Lieut Coyle   But I was about to get rid of them −

Sgt Browne   Here's your passage right enough!

Sgt Browne *reaches under* **Lieut Coyle**'*s long johns, shoving the chain/crucifix up* **Lieut Coyle**'*s arse.*

Lieut Coyle   Aaah!

The **Redcoats** *laugh.*

Capt Farrell (*laughs*)   Oh, forgive me, Father, please!

Sgt Browne   Hand me that prayer book, Farrell!

Capt Farrell (*laughs*)   They know not what they do!

Sgt Browne   Let me anoint it, come on!

Sgt Browne *snatches the prayer book from* **Capt Farrell**. *Over the following, he takes it to the corner of the tavern and pisses on it.*

Lieut Coyle (*to* **Skelton**)   I beg you, please, I didn't −

Capt Skelton *flogs* **Lieut Coyle** *with his sword.*

Capt Skelton   You didn't what?

Lieut Coyle   I didn't think, I didn't think −

Capt Skelton *flogs* **Lieut Coyle** *with his sword.*

Capt Skelton   You didn't think, Coyle, come on!

Lieut Coyle   But I would never in my dreams –

Capt Skelton   You didn't think, Coyle, you didn't think!

He flogs **Lieut Coyle** *several times, bringing him to his knees.*

Lieut Ryan *watches from his chair, uncomfortably smoking his pipe.*

The **Pot-Boy** *continues to bleed to death.*

Capt Skelton   Out with it, man! What, have you lost your tongue?!

Lieut Coyle   I told you, I'm not –

Capt Farrell *and* **Cpl O'Connor** *flog* **Lieut Coyle**.

Lieut Coyle   Jesus save me!

Capt Skelton   Let's hear you, traitor!

Lieut Coyle   Brothers, please, my allegiance is with the King!

Capt Farrell   Would you sing for our King?

Lieut Coyle   I swear to you –

Capt Farrell   Would you sing?

Capt Skelton   Would you sing the Hymn of Old England, would you sing?

Cpl O'Connor   Lieutenant Coyle!

Lieut Coyle   But you know that I wouldn't –

Sgt Browne (*returns with the soaked missal*)   Sing, you damn imposter!

Lieut Coyle   In all our time together, have I ever – ?

Sgt Browne *rips a page from out of the missal and shoves it in* **Lieut Coyle**'s *mouth.*

Sgt Browne   Let's hear you, come on!

Lieut Coyle   Boys, please!

The **Redcoats** *pull* **Lieut Coyle** *to his feet.*

Lieut Coyle   Please, you can't —

Capt Farrell   On your feet!

Lieut Coyle   Don't do this to me, I'm not the one you're after, it's —

Sgt Browne *stuffs the missal into* **Lieut Coyle***'s mouth and throat.*

Sgt Browne   Sing the Hymn of Britannia!

Cpl O'Connor   Sing along, come on!

Redcoats (*sing*)
 God bless our Lord the King!
 God save our Lord the King!
 God save our King!

As they sing, **Lieut Coyle** *struggles to break free, while the* **Redcoats** *flog and jab him with their swords.*

Redcoats (*sing*)
 Make him victorious,
 Happy and glorious,
 Long to reign over us,
 God bless our King!

Lieut Coyle *collapses. They laugh.*

Over the next, **Capt Skelton** *takes* **Lieut Coyle***'s jacket, and drapes it over* **Lieut Ryan***'s shoulders.*

Capt Farrell (*kicks* **Coyle**)   On your feet!

Sgt Browne (*kicks* **Coyle**)   Get up!

Cpl O'Connor (*kicks* **Coyle**)   Get up, Lieutenant!

Sgt Browne (*kicks* **Coyle**)   Prove yourself, come on with you!

Sgt Browne *boots* **Lieut Coyle** *in the face.*

Capt Skelton (*to* **Ryan**)   Your dog seems to have lost his tongue, Lieutenant.

Blackout.

Four

The cabin.

Night.

The storm continues.

Ellen *crouches on the floor.* **Maryanne**, *her face slashed and semi-conscious, has her head resting on her daughter's lap.* **Ellen** *is trying to feed her soup from a bowl.*

Ellen   Mammy.

Pause.

Mammy, please.

Long pause.

Mammy, please, drink up.

Pause.

Drink up.

Pause.

Drink it, Mammy, please, I made it for you.

Thunder and lightning.

Pause.

I cooked it up special, look.

Pause.

I used the blood from out the pig – please, you'll need all the strength you can get.

Thunder and lightning.

Come on, Mammy, the colour's draining from your cheeks.

Pause.

Come on, Mammy, you're not even trying!

She punches **Maryanne**'s *chest.*

Ellen You've got to work harder, please!

*She punches **Maryanne**'s chest.*

Pause.

*She checks **Maryanne**'s heartbeat.*

Long pause.

Ellen That's it.

Pause.

That's it now, open wide.

*She feeds **Maryanne** the soup.*

Ellen Swallow.

Pause.

There's a good mammy, that's right. We'll soon be back on our feet now, won't we?

Pause.

Back on our feet and ready for Daddy's return.

Pause.

Back on our feet for the feast. Ready for Easter, Mammy, that's right, just . . . What?

*She leans into **Maryanne**.*

Ellen What's that?

Pause.

You'll have to speak up, Mammy, I can barely make you out.

Pause.

Has he what?

Pause.

Oh no, I don't think so.

Pause.

No, I don't think he'll be coming back just yet. Not until he's finished packing I shouldn't think.

Pause.

That's right, Mammy, yes. He'll be packing our ball gowns as we speak, imagine that!

Pause.

Imagine that now, won't you? Our beautiful pink ball gowns, Mammy! In our jewels and sweet perfumes! The both of us, look! In our chariot the shape of a swan!

Thunder and lightning.

Enter **Dermot***, clutching onto the roasted piglet. He stands in the doorway of the cabin, unseen by* **Ellen***. The chains remain attached to his ankles, but unfastened, allowing him to move freely.*

Long pause.

Ellen Mammy?

Long pause.

Mammy, wake up.

Dermot We should go now.

Ellen Would you like me to pray for you?

Dermot We should go now, Ellen.

Ellen You'd like that, wouldn't you?

Pause.

Dermot Ellen . . .

Ellen (*recites*) 'And I saw a new heaven and a new earth: for the first heaven and the first earth were passed away; and there was no more sea. And I saw the holy city, new Jerusalem, coming down from God out of heaven, as a bride adorned for her husband. And I heard a great voice out of heaven saying, Behold, the tabernacle of God is with men, and he will dwell with them, and they shall be his people, and God himself shall be with them and be their God.'

Pause.

Ellen/Dermot   'And God shall wipe all the tears away from their eyes; and there shall be no more death, neither sorrow nor crying, neither shall there be any more pain: for the former things are passed away. And he that sat upon the throne said, Behold, I make all things new.'

Thunder and lightning.

Pause.

Ellen (*to* **Maryanne**)   Finish it off now, Mammy, come on.

Long pause.

Dermot   Ellen . . .

Ellen (*to* **Maryanne**)   You want to keep your health for the voyage.

Long pause.

Back on your feet for the Palace, that's it.

Dermot   Ellen . . .

Ellen   Buckingham Palace. You remember how we dreamed of the life to come?

Dermot   Ellen, look at me.

Ellen   Quiet!

Dermot   I think –

Ellen   Quiet, I say!

Dermot   I think we should go now, please.

Ellen *continues feeding* **Maryanne**.

Pause.

Dermot   We should go now, Ellen.

Ellen   Would you let me finish?!

Dermot   But –

Ellen   Let me finish, Dermot – no!

Dermot   They're coming for us.

Ellen   You're not supposed to be here!

Dermot   They're coming for me, listen! They're burning down the cabins, Ellen, will you not see?!

Ellen   Mammy said –

Dermot   Take a look if you don't believe me!

Ellen   Mammy said you're not to be here any more, she said so.

Dermot   But, sister, you're not –

Ellen   You're supposed to be a soldier now, Dermot – go on!

Dermot   Sister, please . . .

Ellen   Don't come near me, I said, you're not welcome!

Long pause.

The stench on you.

Dermot   I'm telling you, Ellen –

Ellen   Did you do it?

Dermot   She's deceived us, I swear.

Ellen   Did you free the pigs?

Dermot   What?

Ellen   Mammy told you to go to the farm, did you free them?

Dermot   Of course!

Ellen   Did you free the chickens?

Pause.

The chickens, Dermot. Did you free them from their blood?

Pause.

Don't make me use the stick.

Dermot   Yes, miss.

Ellen   And the sheep?

Dermot   Yes, miss.

Ellen   And the cows?

Pause.

And the cows, Dermot, answer me!

Dermot   Of course I freed the cows, I freed them all! I freed one just for you here – look!

He offers the piglet to **Ellen.**

Dermot   I freed her for you, Ellen.

Pause.

Look on her, won't you?

Ellen   Fibber.

Dermot   I picked her from the litter especially.

Ellen   You're always fibbing.

Dermot (*as the piglet*)   'Hello, Ellen.'

Ellen   But Mammy said –

Dermot (*as the piglet*)   'Hello, little sweet one. Daisy's the name.' Oh, she is a pretty one though, isn't she? See how she dances – look.

He plays with the piglet.

(*As the piglet.*)   'Hello, little girl-girl, hello, hello, hello. Won't you be my best friend?'

Ellen   Dermot, please . . .

Dermot (*as the piglet*)   'Daisy's the name.'

Ellen   Stop it, I say! That's not funny!

Dermot   But we may take her with us to the bog. We may hide among the reeds together. You'd like that, wouldn't you, Daisy? 'Oh, yes please, Dermot, yes please . . . '

Ellen   Stop lying to me, Dermot!

Dermot   But –

Ellen   It's me she needs . . .

She grabs the piglet off **Dermot**, *clutching on to it.*

Ellen   Leave it alone!

She continues feeding **Maryanne** *while holding the piglet to her chest.*

Long pause.

Dermot   Is she wounded?

Ellen (*to* **Maryanne**)   Mind you don't spill now.

Dermot   He did this to her, didn't he?

Ellen   Mind the wee drippy drops, that's it.

Dermot   It was Daddy, wasn't it?

Ellen   Just a few more . . .

Dermot   Tell me the truth, Ellen! He took his metal to her, didn't he? What, won't you speak? Who did this?!

Ellen   Don't be scared now, Mammy, it's only Dermot.

Dermot   Then I suppose it was the thunder, was it?!

Ellen   There's nothing to be afraid of.

Dermot   The thunder and the lightning struck her down! Is that what you'd like me to believe? I'll believe anything, you know that. It was the thunder, I knew it!

Ellen (*to* **Maryanne**)   That's it, Mammy . . .

Dermot   Is this what you'd like me to believe?!

Ellen   . . . one mouthful at a time.

Dermot   Should we choose the thunder?!

Ellen (*to* **Maryanne**)   Don't you worry about a –

Dermot   Let us believe that, Ellen, let us leave this place! Come on now, it's as good a game as any!

Ellen   You're scaring her.

Dermot   Ellen, please . . .

Ellen   She needs me – stop!

Dermot   It's going to strike every last one of us down, I tell you, we can't stay here!

L-Cpl Finnigan (*off, in the distance*)   Ho there!

Dermot   What, are you deaf? It's getting closer – listen!

L-Cpl Finnigan (*off*)   Show yourself, little bastard you, ho! It's your stink that gives you away!

Dermot *dashes over to* **Ellen.**

Dermot   Oh, won't you come with me, sister?

Ellen   I'm supposed to wait here with my mammy.

Dermot   But we haven't any time.

Ellen   I'm to wait till daybreak.

Dermot (*goes to touch* **Ellen**)   Ellen, please . . .

Ellen   Keep your hands off me! I'm to be a good girl!

Dermot   Won't you listen?!

Ellen   Stay away from me, Dermot!

Dermot   For the good of us both! Look at what they've done to me already! I swear to you, on my heart . . .

Ellen   My heart is with Daddy.

Dermot   Daddy's dead.

Ellen *stops feeding* **Maryanne.**

Long pause.

Ellen *begins plaiting* **Maryanne**'s *hair.*

Dermot   Come and play with me, Ellen, please.

Pause.

We could hide by the bog and watch the storm together.

Pause.

You remember the bog? You remember I used to take you there when you were just a bairn? We could go there now.

Pause.

We could pray to the saints together.

Pause.

We could call upon the Pope. Remember our special prayer?

Pause.

I remember.

Pause.

I remember when we might still walk freely upon this land.

Pause.

I remember how she used to carry me in her arms. And I just a babe. As you are now, Ellen, look.

Pause.

She would carry me to the river and we'd whisper of Saint Ita.

Pause.

She'd whisper me the life to come. Of how we might never face Purgatory. Of how we might yet remain free, no matter what they stole from us. Of how we might never lose sight of each other, Ellen – well?

Long pause.

Let me take you in my arms.

Long pause.

Ellen.

Long pause.

Ellen, please, we may still have each other.

Ellen   But Mammy said so.

Dermot   Mammy is corrupted, look! Look at her! What are you crying for?

Ellen   She promised she would never leave me.

Dermot   Don't you cry for her.

Ellen   But she did, she did!

Dermot   Don't you do it now, child, I'm warning you!

*He tries to pull **Ellen** away from **Maryanne**.*

Dermot   For the love of God, don't –

Ellen   Ow!

Dermot   Don't do this, I swear to you, don't –

Pounding at the cabin door.

Oh Jesus Christ, oh no!

*He leaps onto **Ellen**, covering her mouth.*

Ellen *struggles to break free.*

Dermot   Stay down, will you?!

Ellen   Dermot, please, you're hurting me!

Dermot   Be quiet, Ellen, be quiet!

Ellen   Get off me, you're not –

Pounding at the cabin door.

L-Cpl Finnigan (*off*)   You there, open this door!

Ellen *tries to break free, but **Dermot** suppresses her.*

L-Cpl Finnigan (*off*)   Open this door I say – ho!

Pounding at the cabin door.

Dermot *drags a struggling* **Ellen** *to the cabin door and presses their weight against it.*

L-Cpl Finnigan (*off*)   In the name of our King!

L-Cpl Finnigan, *offstage, tries booting the cabin door open.* **Dermot,** *with* **Ellen,** *keeps the door shut.*

L-Cpl Finnigan (*off*)   Open up, open up!

Thunder and lightning.

Ellen *and* **Dermot** *struggle.*

Dermot   Jesus save us, Ellen! Ellen, please!

Ellen   Stay back, I said!

Dermot   Don't fight with me, not now!

Ellen (*breaks free*)   Stay back, stay back! Mammy, please, they're here!

Ellen *rushes to* **Maryanne** *and tries to wake her.*

Dermot *holds the cabin door shut, as* **L-Cpl Finnigan** *continues to boot it down.*

Ellen   The soldiers have come for us – look! Wake up, Mammy, please!

L-Cpl Finnigan (*off*)   Open the door, you fucking weasel!

Ellen   Won't you live to see our freedom?! I'm telling you, they're –

L-Cpl Finnigan *boots down the door, and enters.*

Ellen   – here, look, they're here!

Dermot (*tries to flee from* **Finnigan**)   You'll not touch me, you beast!

L-Cpl Finnigan (*grabs* **Dermot**)   What, do you go by fucking Abraham or something?!

Dermot   I'm warning you, don't . . . !

L-Cpl Finnigan   That you should escape your own judgement!

Dermot *draws his blade from his pocket.*

L-Cpl Finnigan   That you think you can get past me with your –

Dermot *stabs* **L-Cpl Finnigan** *with his knife.*

Pause.

L-Cpl Finnigan   Oh Jesus, no.

Dermot *stabs* **L-Cpl Finnigan** *twice.*

Pause.

L-Cpl Finnigan   Oh Lucy . . .

Dermot *stabs* **L-Cpl Finnigan** *several more times.*

He falls to the ground.

Thunder and lightning.

Long pause.

Ellen   Dermot –

Dermot   Be silent, Ellen, damn you!

Ellen   But –

Dermot   Silence, I say!

He throws his blade to the ground.

Long pause.

Ellen   But he came to take us away.

Pause.

Dirty murdering –

Dermot   Oh, that's right, Ellen, that's right, you give me that title!

Ellen (*makes for* **Finnigan**)   But he was one of Daddy's friends!

Dermot *bars* **Ellen** *from the dead body, grabbing her. They struggle.*

Dermot   Aye, friend, that's right, and may the flies hatch their eggs in his wound! A thousand filthy maggots, so be it! Might they hatch in his mouth and wriggle their way out through his hole! I'll take any number of them, you hear?! I'll take God Himself so help me!

Ellen   Stop it, I say – let go!

Ellen *breaks free from* **Dermot**, *darting back to* **Maryanne**.

Dermot   That's right, you run right back to her now!

Ellen   You're not in your right mind!

Dermot   Run back to that hag, go on! Go on with you!

Ellen   Dermot, please . . .

Dermot   She who would fail her own son!

Ellen   But that's not it at all!

Dermot   She who would send me to my grave! Who would betray her own word!

Ellen   No, you're wrong!

Dermot   The storm's in her pocket, Ellen, do you think I don't know that?!

Ellen *tends to* **Maryanne**.

Long pause.

Dermot   She's turned the town against itself, look.

Long pause.

Ellen, please, we have to believe that.

Long pause.

We have to believe something.

Long pause.

Look at me.

Ellen No . . .

Dermot Let us believe something. Anything . . .

Ellen God is with us always, Dermot.

Dermot God would never do this to His own kind.

Pause.

Well, would he?

Thunder and lightning.

Long pause.

Come on now, sister, do my words mean nothing to you any more?

Long pause.

Ellen, please . . .

Ellen Let me fasten your chains at least.

Dermot Am I not your brother?

Ellen We can fasten your chains, Dermot, come on!

She removes a padlock and key from **Maryanne**'*s pocket.*

Pause.

Ellen For your own protection.

Dermot Oh . . .

Ellen Come on now, please.

Dermot We can, can't we?

Ellen Let me help you back to the tree.

Dermot We can do that, Ellen, you traitor!

Ellen Please, just −

Dermot We can do just as Mammy says!

Ellen Just stop being so stupid, you know it's for your own good.

Dermot We can fall on our knees and grovel!

Ellen You don't want another murder on your hands.

Dermot Might we do that, sister?

Ellen Look . . .

Dermot What else might we do? Well, come on!

Ellen I'm only trying to help . . .

Dermot Might I be chained to the oak for Mammy to beat me?

Ellen But we can be a family again.

Dermot What, to keep me as a slave to serve her supper? To fetch in wood and keep the vermin at bay? Might I do that, Ellen?

He wrestles the padlock and key from **Ellen**.

Dermot Might I take your stinking key and bind myself at your command?

Ellen Dermot, please!

Dermot Might I do that?

Ellen You're not allowed to do that, don't break the rules.

Dermot Here!

He moves to the post – a tree that forms part of the cabin – and fastens himself to it with the padlock and key.

Let me help you, Ellen, please!

Thunder and lightning.

Let me serve at your command – here I am! Here I am, Ellen! Tied to the post as you bid!

He pulls himself to his feet with difficulty.

Well? What would you have me do, oh Queen? What else would you have me do?

Ellen *returns to* **Maryanne**, *crouching down by her.*

Long pause.

Dermot   What else, Ellen?

Ellen   No.

Dermot   What else?

Ellen   You're not being very fair, Dermot.

Dermot   I'm here for you – look.

Ellen   We can't carry on like this.

Dermot   I'm here for you, Ellen, come on. That I should pay for your sins. That Mammy should make me suffer.

Ellen   We must pray like good girls and boys.

Dermot   Ellen, please! I can choose this madness no longer! What, should I lay down my life to you?! Should I give you my flesh?! My hands and my feet, my nose and my throat! These two pitiful fucking jellies?! Shall I offer them up for you now?!

He clutches his eyeballs with both hands.

Oh, that the earth would swallow me whole! That I would –

He claws and drags the eyes from out of his head.

– never have have been your witness!!

Thunder and lightning.

Long pause.

He kneels on the ground, blinded.

Long pause.

Cpl O'Connor *and* **Lieut Ryan**, *swords drawn, silently enter the cabin, unnoticed by the children.*

Lieut Ryan *moves straight to the body of* **L-Cpl Finnigan** *and crouches down by him.*

Cpl O'Connor *moves to* **Ellen** *and takes her hand.*

Long pause.

Dermot   Ellen.

Cpl O'Connor *leads* **Ellen** *out of the cabin. They exit.*

Lieut Ryan *tries to resuscitate* **L-Cpl Finnigan.**

Maryanne *is beginning to regain consciousness, pulling herself onto all fours.*

Long pause.

Dermot   Ellen.

Pause.

Look on me, girl.

Long pause.

Ellen . . .

Maryanne (*barely conscious*)   You're a good boy, Dermot.

Dermot (*to* **Ellen**)   Won't you look on me?

Maryanne *begins to crawl towards* **Dermot,** *very slowly.*

Long pause.

Dermot   Won't you tell me what to do?

Long pause.

Who else can we tell but each other?

Maryanne *has crawled over to* **Dermot** *and begins undoing his chains.*

Long pause.

Dermot   Ellen, please, I'm begging you!

Lieut Ryan *clubs* **Maryanne** *over the head with the butt of his sword.*

Dermot   Tell me what to do!

Blackout.

Five

Night.

The storm continues outside, clearly audible.

Col Fleming's *quarters – austere and elegant, candlelit.*

Col Fleming, *an Englishman, is sitting at his desk, slowly reading through a parchment.*

Lieut Coyle, *battered and bruised, stands at a distance before* **Col Fleming**. *In front of* **Lieut Coyle** *is an empty chair.*

Sgt Browne, **Capt Farrell** *and* **Capt Skelton** *stand in a line, behind* **Col Fleming**.

Col Fleming   What should we do with him?

Lieut Coyle   I couldn't say, sir.

Long pause.

Col Fleming   Are you uncomfortable?

Long pause.

Lieutenant Coyle . . .

Lieut Coyle   I don't think I understand the question, sir.

Col Fleming   You're hard of hearing?

Lieut Coyle   No, Colonel, I . . .

Col Fleming   Should I raise my voice for you?

Lieut Coyle   Uncomfortable.

Col Fleming   What?

Lieut Coyle   A little, sir, yes.

Pause.

The boys were somewhat rough with me, I'd say.

Col Fleming   They were.

Lieut Coyle   Yes . . .

Col Fleming   That's understandable.

Lieut Coyle   Yes, sir.

Pause.

Perfectly.

Col Fleming   What?

Lieut Coyle   They were . . .

Col Fleming   Your boys are grieving for their homeland, are they not?

Lieut Coyle   Yes.

Pause.

Yes, possibly . . .

Col Fleming   Am I hearing things, Sergeant Browne?

Sgt Browne   A mutter, Colonel.

Col Fleming   Oh.

Sgt Browne   I believe the Lieutenant muttered something.

Col Fleming   I see.

Sgt Browne   Under his breath.

Lieut Coyle   They had good reason, sir.

Col Fleming   Thank you, Sergeant.

Lieut Coyle   They were perfectly within their rights, I mean.

Col Fleming   Yes.

Lieut Coyle   Colonel, please –

Col Fleming   Yes, that's –

Lieut Coyle   If you would just let me explain –

Col Fleming   That's much more like it, Coyle, but you don't have to shout the whole house down.

He continues reading the parchment.

Long pause.

You were recruited at eighteen.

Lieut Coyle   Yes, sir.

Col Fleming   Though you come from a Catholic family.

Lieut Coyle   Well . . .

Col Fleming   It says here your brother was executed.

Lieut Coyle   That's correct, yes.

Pause.

A fortnight after your arrival, sir.

Pause.

He bought a horse for over five pounds.

Col Fleming   He was a farmer.

Lieut Coyle   Yes.

Col Fleming   He and his wife owned . . .

Lieut Coyle   The farm you've occupied these past twenty years, Colonel, yes.

Col Fleming   A man of property, yes?

Lieut Coyle   Moderate, yes, I suppose.

Col Fleming   How very interesting.

Long pause.

Lieut Coyle   Colonel, please, if you think that I had any hand –

Col Fleming   It doesn't seem particularly fair, though.

Lieut Coyle   Sir.

Col Fleming   To take a man's life for the sale of a horse.

Lieut Coyle   I don't –

Col Fleming   Is that fair?

Lieut Coyle   He broke the law, sir.

Col Fleming   So it would seem.

Pause.

And his wife?

Lieut Coyle   Yes, sir.

Col Fleming   You bore her children.

Lieut Coyle   Every man has his vice, sir.

Col Fleming   Well said.

Pause.

Lieut Coyle   Forgive me, but . . .

Col Fleming   There are certain pleasures your own wife cannot give, yes?

Lieut Coyle   Well . . .

Col Fleming   The curse of familiarity.

Lieut Coyle   As much as any man.

Col Fleming   Though you have married into considerable wealth.

Lieut Coyle   I do not doubt her charity, sir.

Col Fleming   I know her family well.

Lieut Coyle   They speak highly of you, sir.

Col Fleming   Munitions.

Lieut Coyle   That's right, yes.

Col Fleming   And you would jeopardise this wealth?

Long pause.

Are you unhappy, Lieutenant?

Lieut Coyle   Possibly, sir.

Col Fleming   Just 'possibly'?

Lieut Coyle   Yes. Yes, I mean . . .

Col Fleming   I'm surprised you're not hanging from one of our trees.

Lieut Coyle   I am your servant, sir.

Col Fleming   I dare say you could lose some weight. Are you fit enough to go into war, do you think?

Lieut Coyle   Oh . . .

Col Fleming   One very much doubts it.

Lieut Coyle   Yes, sir, of course.

Col Fleming   We leave in two days' time, I –

Lieut Coyle   Irrefutably, Your Honour.

Col Fleming   What?

Lieut Coyle   Of course, I mean –

Col Fleming   Speak up, Lieutenant!

Lieut Coyle (*salutes*)   For His Majesty the King, sir, yes!

Long pause.

Lieut Coyle *remains saluting while* **Col Fleming** *again returns to the parchment.*

Long pause.

Col Fleming   Perhaps you need time to rest.

Long pause.

Perhaps we've expected too much from you.

Lieut Coyle   I don't know what you mean . . .

Col Fleming   As you were, Lieutenant.

Lieut Coyle (*salutes*)   Sir!

Long pause.

Col Fleming   What do you say, Captain?

Capt Farrell I would post his head to London.

Long pause.

Col Fleming Skelton?

Capt Skelton On a pike, sir, yes.

Col Fleming Though I would very much like to meet this family of his.

Long pause.

You do then know the penalty for sedition?

Lieut Coyle Yes, Your Honour, I do.

Col Fleming Yet you feel responsible for this man.

Lieut Coyle He is my son, sir.

Col Fleming Under the authority of Rome.

Pause.

Lieut Coyle Colonel, please, you must know –

Col Fleming (*to* **Farrell**) Do we have a confession yet, Farrell?

Capt Farrell I have it with me here, sir.

Lieut Coyle The boy didn't know what he was doing.

Capt Farrell *passes* **Col Fleming** *a scroll.*

Lieut Coyle He needs a doctor, that's all, sir, he's . . .

Col Fleming *reads the scroll.*

Lieut Coyle He's not in his right mind, I . . .

Pause.

He was drunk, sir, he'd say anything to –

Col Fleming You are of course entitled to appeal on his behalf.

He passes the scroll to **Capt Farrell,** *who then passes it to* **Lieut Coyle.**

Capt Farrell *moves back to his post while* **Lieut Coyle** *reads the parchment.*

Long pause.

Lieut Coyle   Of course, sir, yes.

Col Fleming   Although you would have to stand trial yourself.

Long pause.

Perhaps you sympathise with these people.

Long pause.

Perhaps you think we have no place in this country of yours.

Long pause.

Civilisation is a process, Lieutenant. It can take years. Generations even. I doubt our own grandchildren will live to see the fulfilment of our project. What we do here has repercussions that go beyond anything you or I can imagine. After all, you've proved you're quite capable of adopting our language. I'm equally sure you can assist in the reformation of your parliament when the time comes. But as you people seem unable to rise above the so-called inequalities of the past, our presence here should remain intact, should it not?

Lieut Coyle   Yes, sir.

Col Fleming   Yours is a nation bred for slavery.

Lieut Coyle   Yes, I see.

Col Fleming   It sits at the very roots of your culture. You excel at it.

Lieut Coyle   Thank you.

Col Fleming   St Patrick was an Englishman, Lieutenant.

Pause.

Well?

Long pause.

I had hoped you would have embraced the benefits of service by now. You're quite an inspiration to the men.

Lieut Coyle   It is an honour, of course.

Col Fleming   What should we do with him?

Blackout.

Six

The mud cabin.

Night.

A storm – thunder, lightning and heavy rain.

Maryanne *is sitting on the stool by the peat fire, her back to* **Col Fleming**. *Her face is scarred.*

Col Fleming *is sitting on the edge of the bed, semi-naked. His back and face are scratched, and his wig is removed.*

Lieut Coyle *and* **Lieut Ryan** *guard the cabin door.*

Long pause.

Maryanne   Was everything to your satisfaction, sir?

Long pause.

You're not frightened of the thunder, I hope?

Long pause.

Colonel Fleming, sir . . .

Col Fleming   I'm fine.

Maryanne   Oh.

Pause.

Oh, then maybe your men here would –

Col Fleming   Be quiet.

Maryanne   Yes, sir.

Pause.

Of course, sir.

Long pause.

She lays peat on the fire.

Col Fleming *reaches for his uniform.*

Pause.

He reaches into the pocket of his uniform and removes a drinking flask.

He unscrews the top and takes a drink.

Pause.

He goes to take a second drink.

Maryanne   There's to be quite the storm, I feel.

Col Fleming   There is.

Maryanne   You should feel the way it batters against this old door. You'd think the four horsemen were trying to break in. You'd think the very earth was split in two.

Col Fleming   I can't say I ever pitied a door before.

Maryanne   She is terrified of the thunder. The girl, I mean. She thinks it's out to get her. The thunder and lightning, she thinks it's holding a grudge somehow.

Col Fleming   It can be quite frightening, I imagine.

Maryanne   Well, I don't know where she gets it.

Col Fleming   No.

Maryanne   Though we can none of us hold our fears to ransom, can we, sir?

Pause.

It was spiders with me. Do you like spiders?

Col Fleming   Not particularly.

Maryanne   Do you need more time, sir?

Col Fleming   What?

Maryanne   Would you like me to go back outside?

Long pause.

Maryanne *hands* **Col Fleming** *his wig from the floor. He puts the wig on and takes a drink from the flask.*

Long pause.

Maryanne   I pity that poor horse of yours, Colonel. It can't be good for her, left stranded out there in the cold.

Col Fleming   He should manage, miss.

Maryanne   Would you like me to take him a small blanket?

Pause.

Not that it would provide him much shelter, of course. There's little mercy spared for these hills, sir. There's little life left at all.

Col Fleming   I'm sorry to hear that.

Maryanne   There hasn't one leaf grown from this tree since I last cared remember. I haven't seen so much as a rabbit in years. Not even a priest.

Col Fleming   A pity.

Maryanne   Not a Jesuit, sir, no. They'd sooner brave hanging.

Pause.

Maryanne   They'd sooner brave the lamb, sir.

Long pause.

Will you be riding back to town tonight?

Col Fleming   I expect so, yes.

Maryanne   I could take it off your bill.

Col Fleming   What?

Maryanne   The thunder and lightning.

Pause.

If it's disturbed you, that is.

Long pause.

Although I don't mean to suggest . . .

Col Fleming   That's very kind of you, miss.

Maryanne   I hope you don't think it too forward of me.

Col Fleming   You're not forward.

Maryanne   You were gone an awful long time.

Pause.

You were gone a good while, sir, yes.

Long pause.

Would you like me to clean your wounds for you?

Col Fleming   I'm sorry?

Maryanne   You're bleeding, sir.

Col Fleming   Oh . . .

Maryanne   I might clean your wounds for you.

Long pause.

She remained courteous, I hope.

Long pause.

She remained courteous . . .

Col Fleming   Yes.

Maryanne   Are you sure you're not too cold? I could always lay more turf on the fire.

Pause.

It's no trouble, sir . . .

Col Fleming   Here.

Maryanne   What?

Col Fleming   Take it.

Col Fleming *offers* **Maryanne** *his flask.*

Maryanne   Oh . . .

Col Fleming   Take it.

Maryanne   Oh no, Your Honour, I didn't mean –

Col Fleming   Go on.

Pause.

Maryanne *takes the flask.*

Maryanne   May God protect you, sir.

She drinks from the flask.

Pause.

She goes to hand the flask back . . .

She takes a drink from the flask.

Pause.

She hesitates.

Pause.

She hands the flask back to **Col Fleming**.

Maryanne   Thank you, Colonel.

Pause.

Colonel Fleming, sir . . .

Col Fleming   Forgive me.

Maryanne   What?

Col Fleming   Forgive me.

Long pause.

Maryanne   Well, that is very decent of you, sir, thank you.

She pockets the flask of whisky.

Long pause.

Dead pig, sir.

Col Fleming   Sorry?

Maryanne   Dead pig.

Pause.

A little bacon, sir.

Col Fleming   Thank you, no.

Pause.

Maryanne   Oh well then, maybe . . .

Col Fleming   It is custom for the servant to dress her master.

Maryanne   It is?

Pause.

Oh . . .

Col Fleming   I thought you'd be accustomed to such duties.

Maryanne   Oh, yes . . .

Col Fleming   If you're concerned with payment . . .

Maryanne   Oh, good God . . .

Col Fleming   I am an honourable man . . .

Maryanne   Maryanne, sir.

Col Fleming   . . . Maryanne.

Maryanne   Might you care to stand up?

Pause.

Col Fleming *stands up.*

Long pause.

Maryanne (*remains seated*)   I'm sure she won't be long now, sir.

Long pause.

Maryanne   Ellen.

Pause.

Ellen.

Long pause.

Come on now, Ellen.

She moves to the head of the bed.

Come on now, Ellen, the Colonel's waiting for you.

She peers under the blankets on the bed.

Long pause.

She replaces the blankets.

Long pause.

She begins to silently dress **Col Fleming**.

Long pause.

Lieut Ryan *moves to the corner of the cabin and takes a shovel that is propped up against the wall.*

Lieut Ryan *offers the shovel to* **Lieut Coyle**.

Lieut Ryan   Well, go on.

Pause.

Take it, Lieutenant.

Lieut Coyle   Yes, sir.

Pause.

He takes the shovel.

Lieut Ryan *returns to guard the cabin door.*

Pause.

Lieut Coyle *finds a suitable space on the cabin floor. He begins digging a hole in the cabin floor.*

Maryanne *dresses* **Col Fleming** *and* **Lieut Coyle** *digs the hole.*

Long pause.

Maryanne   Will you be sailing tomorrow morning, sir?

Col Fleming   That's right.

Maryanne   You must be looking forward to seeing your family.

Col Fleming   Yes.

Maryanne   Not that we . . .

Pause.

Begging your pardon, sir.

Col Fleming   Go on.

Maryanne   We will all be sorry to see you go, of course.

Pause.

She continues dressing **Col Fleming**.

Maryanne   Will you be sailing to Europe with your regiment?

Col Fleming   Of course.

Maryanne   Then I shall pray for you, sir.

Long pause.

She finishes dressing **Col Fleming**, *apart from his boots. He moves to the stool by the fire and sits down.*

Pause.

Maryanne *takes the boots from by the fire, then kneels down before* **Col Fleming**.

Pause.

She begins to put the boots on **Col Fleming**.

Col Fleming   You have a very beautiful country.

Maryanne (*stops*)   Sorry, sir?

Col Fleming   The land.

Maryanne   Oh . . .

Col Fleming   You have very beautiful land.

Maryanne   Oh, we do.

Col Fleming   I shall miss the long walks.

Maryanne   We shall miss you, sir.

Pause.

Maryanne *proceeds to put* **Col Fleming**'s *boots on.*

As she does this, **Lieut Coyle** *finishes digging the hole.*

He moves over to the small makeshift bed and pulls back the blankets. He picks up and carries **Ellen**'s *body to the hole. He lays* **Ellen**'s *body in the hole.*

Pause.

Lieut Coyle *begins burying* **Ellen** *as* **Maryanne** *finishes with* **Col Fleming**'s *boots.*

Long pause.

Maryanne   Will that be all, Colonel?

Col Fleming   That's all.

Maryanne   Are they tight enough for you?

Col Fleming   Thank you.

Maryanne *remains kneeling.*

Long pause.

Maryanne (*goes to stand*)   Well . . .

Col Fleming   Oh.

Maryanne (*kneels*)   Yes, sir.

Col Fleming   My debt.

Pause.

He takes the purse from his uniform. He counts a small number of coins from the purse, and hands them to **Maryanne**.

Col Fleming   You may want to count it.

Maryanne *counts the coins.*

Pause.

Maryanne   Thank you, Colonel.

Lieut Coyle *continues burying* **Ellen.**

Long pause.

Maryanne   If there's anything more I can do.

Long pause.

If there's anything you need for your journey, sir.

Long pause.

If I might offer my service.

Pause.

If you're in need of a servant.

Col Fleming   I might.

Maryanne   For the voyage ahead, I mean.

Pause.

Forgive me if I'm being too forward.

Long pause.

Col Fleming   Do you renounce your Pope?

Maryanne   I spit on his cunt.

Long pause.

Him and all his high priests.

Col Fleming   I trust you don't mean . . .

Maryanne   Jesus Christ, sir.

Col Fleming   Oh.

Pause.

Maryanne   Redemption is a lie told by writers and bureaucrats. There are those that lean out the pulpit, and they may speak awful sweet. The life to be. Of epiphany and liberation. But they're no different to them that stand in office. Offering hope when it's truth what's needed. Truth being no more than murder.

Col Fleming   I see.

Maryanne   He can rot in the earth with the rest of us.

Long pause.

The only virtue I crave, sir, is constancy.

Long pause.

Maryanne *offers* **Col Fleming** *his gloves from by the fire.*

Maryanne   You might sell me your horse.

Col Fleming   What?

Maryanne   You might sell me your horse.

Col Fleming *takes his gloves.*

Pause.

Maryanne   You might do that, sir.

Col Fleming   I might.

Maryanne   You could do that for me, sir, yes.

Col Fleming *sits on the stool as he puts on his gloves.*

Maryanne *remains kneeling.*

Long pause.

Col Fleming   Go on.

Maryanne   You could buy back my cattle.

Long pause.

My farm. You could buy back my farm.

Long pause.

What else could you do for me, Colonel?

Lieut Coyle *continues burying* **Ellen.**

Maryanne   What else? Tell me. What else?

Blackout.

Seven

Dawn.

The storm receding: heavy rain, turning light, and the sun slowly rising.

The patch of grassland, before the town gates.

Dermot *is in the stocks.*

Ellen *is sitting on the grass, a distance apart from* **Dermot.**

The **Fiddler** *and the* **Piper** *sit on the grass, a distance apart from them both.*

Long pause.

Ellen   A dozen eyes, you say?

Dermot   A dozen.

Ellen   Oh.

Dermot   A dozen dozen.

Ellen   That's just terrible, isn't it?

Long pause.

Dermot Did you see him?

Pause.

Ellen.

Pause.

You saw him, didn't you, girl?

Long pause.

Ellen . . .

Ellen Great long fangs he has.

Dermot What?

Ellen Great huge fangs.

Dermot No!

Ellen Snarling and foaming like a bear. Wielding his sword.

Dermot One from every other hand. Calling on my submission, the brute.

Ellen That's right, Dermot, yes.

Dermot To think he could do this to his own kind.

Ellen Oh, he was a terrible-sounding Devil all right.

Dermot Didn't I tell you, Ellen?

Pause.

I told you, didn't I?

Ellen Oh, yes . . .

Dermot Then you must've been scared to death.

Ellen Yes, I was.

Dermot I know I would.

Long pause.

Dermot   Ellen . . .

Ellen   Of course, I told him you were sleeping.

Dermot   Did you?

Ellen   He's not to be disturbed, I said. 'Don't you be bothering him, you old bastard!'

Dermot   You didn't!

Ellen   'You leave him alone, you cruel beast! Get down under the earth where you belong! Get down, I tell you, don't you be bothering my brother!'

Long pause.

That'll teach him, won't it?

Dermot   It will.

Ellen   That'll teach him.

Dermot   You're a good girl, Ellen.

Long pause.

The **Fiddler** *and* **Piper** *begin to play a hymn as the sun rises.*

Long pause.

Dermot   Ellen . . .

Ellen   Quiet now, that's enough.

Pause.

Ellen *stands and moves over to* **Dermot.**

She removes a hunk of bread from her pocket.

She climbs onto the small stool by the stocks.

She tears a piece of bread from the hunk and feeds it to **Dermot.**

Long pause.

Ellen   Of course, it'll all turn right in the end.

Long pause.

It'll all turn right, Dermot, yes.

Dermot   Will it?

Ellen   Of course.

Dermot   Oh . . .

Ellen   Yes, of course it will, don't be silly.

She climbs down off the stool. She takes her cloth and bucket and washes **Dermot**.

Long pause.

Ellen   You might grant me that, no?

Pause.

Ellen   Dermot . . .

Dermot   It'll all turn right, Ellen.

Ellen   Daddy promised to speak to the man.

Dermot   Who?

Ellen   The good man.

Dermot   You mean Jesus.

Ellen   No, stupid. The English-speaking man.

Dermot   Was Jesus not English?

Ellen   The man takes care of Daddy, you know. The man who's going to take us away.

Dermot   Where?

Ellen   On the boat of course.

Dermot   Oh.

Ellen   The boat sailing for England.

Long pause.

You remember, don't you, Dermot?

Long pause.

Dermot . . .

Dermot   I remember, child.

Ellen   You believe me though, don't you?

Ellen *rinses the blood from the cloth into the bucket.*

Long pause.

And then we'll be all right, you'll see.

Pause.

And then we'll be free.

Lights fade.

Methuen Drama Modern Plays

include work by

Edward Albee
Jean Anouilh
John Arden
Margaretta D'Arcy
Peter Barnes
Sebastian Barry
Brendan Behan
Dermot Bolger
Edward Bond
Bertolt Brecht
Howard Brenton
Anthony Burgess
Simon Burke
Jim Cartwright
Caryl Churchill
Noël Coward
Lucinda Coxon
Sarah Daniels
Nick Darke
Nick Dear
Shelagh Delaney
David Edgar
David Eldridge
Dario Fo
Michael Frayn
John Godber
Paul Godfrey
David Greig
John Guare
Peter Handke
David Harrower
Jonathan Harvey
Iain Heggie
Declan Hughes
Terry Johnson
Sarah Kane
Charlotte Keatley
Barrie Keeffe
Howard Korder

Robert Lepage
Doug Lucie
Martin McDonagh
John McGrath
Terrence McNally
David Mamet
Patrick Marber
Arthur Miller
Mtwa, Ngema & Simon
Tom Murphy
Phyllis Nagy
Peter Nichols
Sean O'Brien
Joseph O'Connor
Joe Orton
Louise Page
Joe Penhall
Luigi Pirandello
Stephen Poliakoff
Franca Rame
Mark Ravenhill
Philip Ridley
Reginald Rose
Willy Russell
Jean-Paul Sartre
Sam Shepard
Wole Soyinka
Simon Stephens
Shelagh Stephenson
Peter Straughan
C. P. Taylor
Theatre de Complicite
Theatre Workshop
Sue Townsend
Judy Upton
Timberlake Wertenbaker
Roy Williams
Snoo Wilson
Victoria Wood

Methuen Drama Contemporary Dramatists

include

John Arden (two volumes)
Arden & D'Arcy
Peter Barnes (three volumes)
Sebastian Barry
Dermot Bolger
Edward Bond (eight volumes)
Howard Brenton
 (two volumes)
Richard Cameron
Jim Cartwright
Caryl Churchill
 (two volumes)
Sarah Daniels (two volumes)
Nick Darke
David Edgar (three volumes)
David Eldridge
Ben Elton
Dario Fo (two volumes)
Michael Frayn (three volumes)
John Godber (three volumes)
Paul Godfrey
David Greig
John Guare
Lee Hall (two volumes)
Peter Handke
Jonathan Harvey
 (two volumes)
Declan Hughes
Terry Johnson (three volumes)
Sarah Kane
Barrie Keeffe
Bernard-Marie Koltès
 (two volumes)
David Lan
Bryony Lavery
Deborah Levy
Doug Lucie

David Mamet (four volumes)
Martin McDonagh
Duncan McLean
Anthony Minghella
 (two volumes)
Tom Murphy (five volumes)
Phyllis Nagy
Anthony Neilson
Philip Osment
Gary Owen
Louise Page
Stewart Parker (two volumes)
Joe Penhall
Stephen Poliakoff
 (three volumes)
David Rabe
Mark Ravenhill
Christina Reid
Philip Ridley
Willy Russell
Eric-Emmanuel Schmitt
Ntozake Shange
Sam Shepard (two volumes)
Wole Soyinka (two volumes)
Simon Stephens
Shelagh Stephenson
David Storey (three volumes)
Sue Townsend
Judy Upton
Michel Vinaver
 (two volumes)
Arnold Wesker (two volumes)
Michael Wilcox
Roy Williams (two volumes)
Snoo Wilson (two volumes)
David Wood (two volumes)
Victoria Wood

Printed in the USA
CPSIA information can be obtained
at www.ICGtesting.com
LVHW020842171024
794056LV00002B/338

9 781408 101490